Skill Sharpeners 1
for ESL Students

Judy DeFilippo
Charles Skidmore
Michael Walker

ADDISON-WESLEY PUBLISHING COMPANY

Reading, Massachusetts • Menlo Park, California
Don Mills, Ontario • Wokingham, England • Amsterdam • Bonn
Sydney • Singapore • Tokyo • Madrid • Bogota • Santiago • San Juan

Judy DeFilippo is Coordinator of ESL in the Intensive English program at Northeastern University.

Charles Skidmore is an ESL teacher at the secondary level in the Boston, Massachusetts, schools.

Michael Walker is the author of *New Horizons in English, Yes!, Step Ahead,* and other ESL series and texts.

Illustrations by Kathleen Todd: pp. 9, 10, 11, 12, 13, 17, 21, 22, 23, 26, 27, 29, 34, 35, 36, 40, 43, 44, 45, 47, 49, 51, 53, 55, 56, 60, 61, 62, 65, 66, 69, 72, 73, 74, 75, 77, 79, 85, 91, 92, 97, 98, 100, 101, 103, 108, 111, 114

Other illustrations by Dave Blanchette and Susan Avishi

Cover design by Marshall Henrichs and Richard Hannus

IJ-WC-89
ISBN: 0-201-15623-7

Introduction

The *Skill Sharpeners* series has been especially designed for Junior High and Senior High School students who are coping with a new language and a new culture. By introducing basic skills tied to classroom subjects, in a simple, easy-to-understand ESL grammatical framework, the series helps to bridge the gap between ESL and regular academic subjects. By developing and reinforcing school and life survival skills, it helps build student confidence and success. Although designed specifically to accompany the Second Edition of *New Horizons in English*, the *Skill Sharpeners* can be used to supplement and complement any basic ESL series. They may also be used to reteach and reinforce specific skills with which students are having difficulty; to review and practice grammatical structures; and to reinforce, expand, and enrich students' vocabularies.

The grammatical structures in the *Skill Sharpeners* reflect the systematic, small-step progression that is a key feature of the *New Horizons* textbooks. The vocabulary and skill presentation, however, expand the text material with concepts and situations that have an immediate impact on students' daily lives and with themes and subject matter directly related to curriculum areas. Reading and study skills are stressed in many pages, and writing skills are carefully developed, starting with single words and sentences and building gradually to paragraphs and stories in a structured controlled-composition sequence.

You will find that some pages deviate from the structural presentation in the *New Horizons* texts in order accurately to present their important content. You should not expect most students to be able actively to use the structures on these pages in speaking or writing, but students should, however, be able to read and respond to the content. Do not be concerned about structural errors during discussion of the material. It is important that students become *actively involved* and *communicating*, however imperfectly, from the very beginning.

Using the *Skill Sharpeners*

Because each page of the *Skill Sharpeners* books is independent and self contained, the series lends itself to great flexibility in use. Teachers may pick and choose pages that fit the needs of particular students, or they may use the pages in sequential order. Most pages are self explanatory, and all are easy to use, either in class or as homework assignments. Detailed annotations on each page identify the skill or skills being developed and suggest ways to prepare for, introduce, and present the exercise(s) on the page. In most cases, oral practice of the material is suggested before the student is asked to complete the page in writing. Teacher demonstration and student involvement and participation help build a foundation for completing the page successfully and learning the skill.

3

The *Skill Sharpeners* are divided into units corresponding to the units of the *New Horizons* texts. In addition, each of the *Skill Sharpeners* books opens with a review/transition/orientation unit. In *Skill Sharpeners 1*, this is called "Getting Started" and provides introductory exercises to familiarize students with basic classroom language, school deportment, the names of various school areas and school personnel, number names, time and calendar names, and words for feelings and common requests. In later books of the series, the introductory unit serves both to review some of the material taught in earlier books and to provide orientation for students coming to the school or to the series for the first time.

At the end of each of the *Skill Sharpeners* books is a review of vocabulary and an end-of-book test of grammatical and reading skills. The test, in multiple-choice format, not only assesses learning of the skills but also serves as practice for other multiple-choice tests. The use of multiple-choice questions is developed in a number of the exercises in the first *Skill Sharpeners* book and is reinforced in the later books in the series.

The complete Table of Contents in each book identifies the skills developed on each page. A Skills Index at the end of the book lists skills alphabetically and indicates the pages on which they are developed.

Skill Sharpeners invite expansion! We encourage you to use them as a springboard and to add activities and exercises that build on those in the books to fill the needs of your own particular students. Used this way, the *Skill Sharpeners* can significantly help to build the confidence and skills that students need to be successful members of their new community and successful achievers in their subject-area classrooms.

Contents

UNIT 3　Time and Place

UNIT 4　Describing People

UNIT 5　Food and Drink

UNIT 6　Occupations and Nationalities

Contents

UNIT 11　Chores and Pleasures

UNIT 12　Health, the Weather, and Social Engagements

Classroom Language

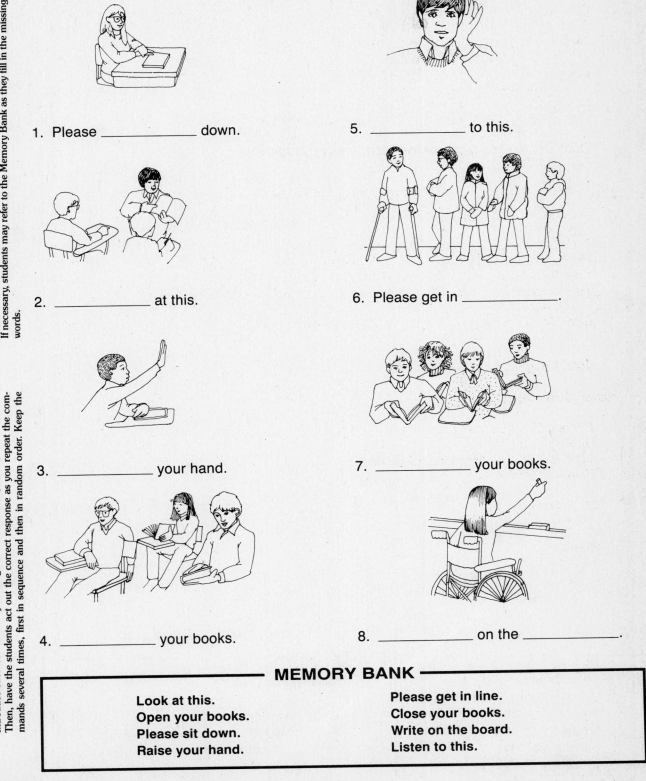

1. Please _____ down.

2. _____ at this.

3. _____ your hand.

4. _____ your books.

5. _____ to this.

6. Please get in _____.

7. _____ your books.

8. _____ on the _____.

MEMORY BANK

Look at this.
Open your books.
Please sit down.
Raise your hand.

Please get in line.
Close your books.
Write on the board.
Listen to this.

Things to Remember

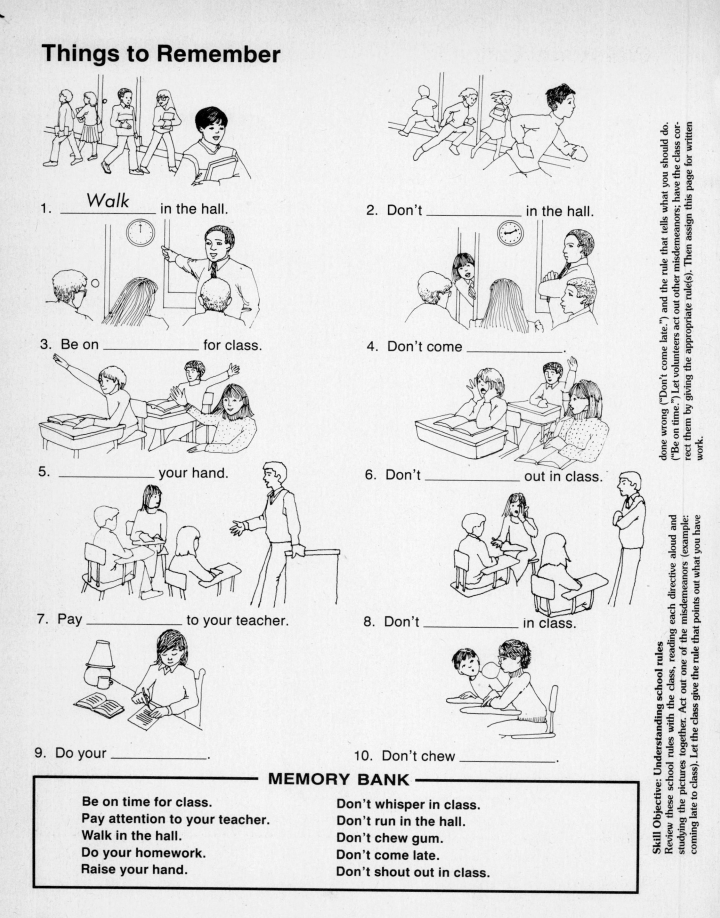

1. _____*Walk*_____ in the hall.

2. Don't _____ in the hall.

3. Be on _____ for class.

4. Don't come _____ .

5. _____ your hand.

6. Don't _____ out in class.

7. Pay _____ to your teacher.

8. Don't _____ in class.

9. Do your _____ .

10. Don't chew _____ .

──── MEMORY BANK ────

Be on time for class.
Pay attention to your teacher.
Walk in the hall.
Do your homework.
Raise your hand.

Don't whisper in class.
Don't run in the hall.
Don't chew gum.
Don't come late.
Don't shout out in class.

Skill Objective: Understanding school rules
Review these school rules with the class, reading each directive aloud and studying the pictures together. Act out one of the misdemeanors (example: coming late to class). Let the class give the rule that points out what you have done wrong ("Don't come late.") and the rule that tells what you should do. ("Be on time.") Let volunteers act out other misdemeanors; have the class correct them by giving the appropriate rule(s). Then assign this page for written work.

Which Way?

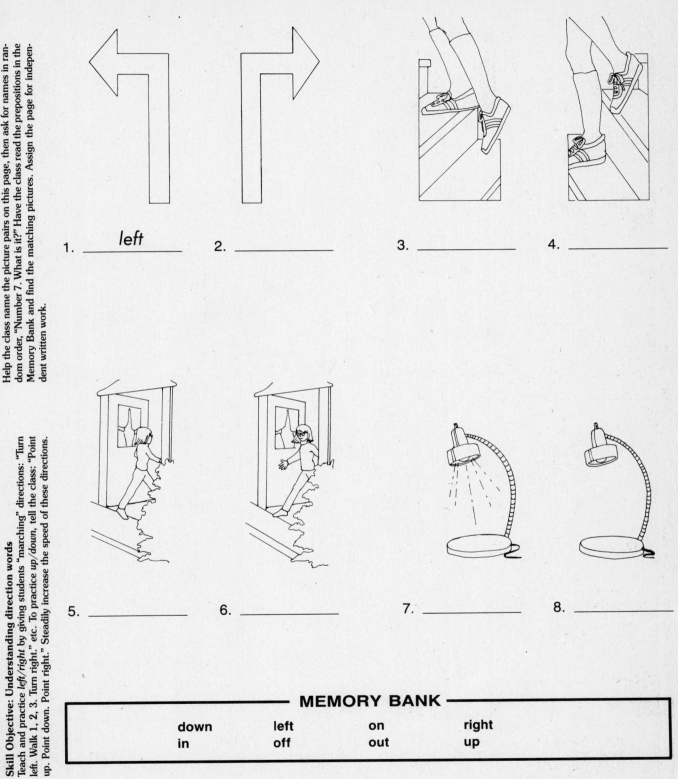

Help the class name the picture pairs on this page, then ask for names in random order, "Number 7. What is it?" Have the class read the prepositions in the Memory Bank and find the matching pictures. Assign the page for independent written work.

1. _left_

2. _____

3. _____

4. _____

Skill Objective: Understanding direction words
Teach and practice *left/right* by giving students "marching" directions: "Turn left. Walk 1, 2, 3. Turn right." etc. To practice *up/down*, tell the class: "Point up. Point down. Point right." Steadily increase the speed of these directions.

5. _____

6. _____

7. _____

8. _____

MEMORY BANK

down	left	on	right
in	off	out	up

Skill Sharpeners 1—Getting Started

At School

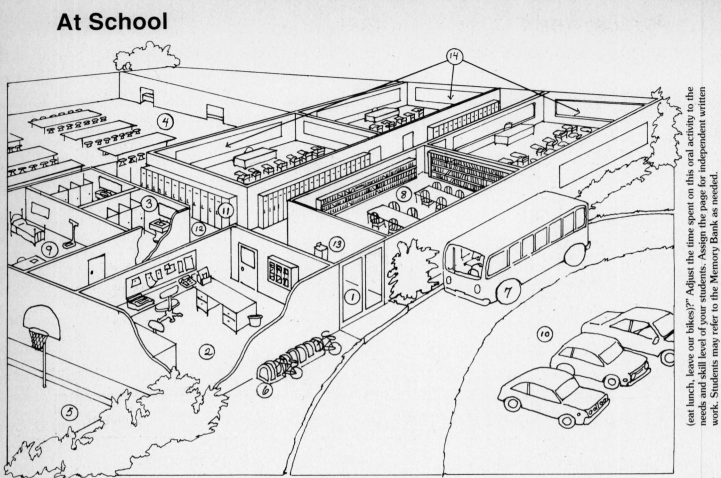

(eat lunch, leave our bikes)?" Adjust the time spent on this oral activity to the needs and skill level of your students. Assign the page for independent written work. Students may refer to the Memory Bank as needed.

Skill Objectives: Naming school rooms and locations, reading a map. Help students identify the fourteen locations highlighted on the school map. Provide practice with the terms by asking: "Where is the (office)? (It's number ___.) 2.) Do we have an (office) in our school? What is number . . .? Where do we

Find the number in the picture. Write the word on the line.

1. _entrance_

2. _____

3. _____

4. _____

5. _____

6. _____

7. _____

8. _____

9. _____

10. _____

11. _____

12. _____

13. _____

14. _____

MEMORY BANK

bathroom	bike rack	classrooms	hallway
library	lockers	lunchroom	nurse's office
office	parking lot	playground	school bus
water fountain		entrance	

People and Places at School

A. Who is she? Who is he? Write the words. The first one is done for you.

1. *principal*

2. _____

3. _____

4. _____

5. _____

6. _____

MEMORY BANK

| bus driver | gym teacher | librarian | math teacher | nurse | principal |

B. Where is he? Where is she? Write the words. The first one is done for you.

1. *playground*

2. _____

3. _____

4. _____

5. _____

6. _____

MEMORY BANK

| classroom | library | nurse's office | hallway | lunchroom | playground |

Number Names

0 zero	1 one	2 two	3 three	4 four	5 five	6 six	7 seven	8 eight	9 nine	10 ten

11 eleven	12 twelve	13 thirteen	14 fourteen	15 fifteen	16 sixteen	17 seventeen

18 eighteen	19 nineteen	20 twenty	21 twenty-one	30 thirty	40 forty	50 fifty	60 sixty

70 seventy	80 eighty	90 ninety	100 one hundred	101 one hundred one	1000 one thousand

A. Write the number names.

1 _one_____

19 _____

5 _____

300 _____

20 _____

90 _____

3 _____

17 _____

201 _____

220 _____

88 _____

308 _____

6000 _____

70 _____

33 _____

B. Write the numbers.

twenty-seven _27_____

forty-three _____

nine _____

one hundred five _____

C. Write the number names in the boxes.

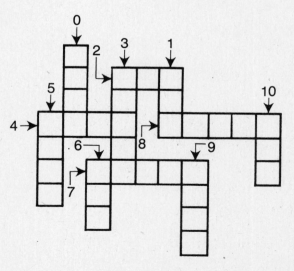

Skill Objective: Naming numbers 1-10,000
Use any or all of the following introductory activities. 1. Have students count from 1-100, either in chorus or in sequence, going around the room. If possible, display a number chart. 2. Write random numbers on the board for volunteers to name. 3. Name a number 1-10,000. Have students write the numeral at their desks. Write the answer on the board so that students can immediately check and correct their work. Review directions and assign this page for independent work.

What Time Is It?

Write the sentence. The first one is done for you.

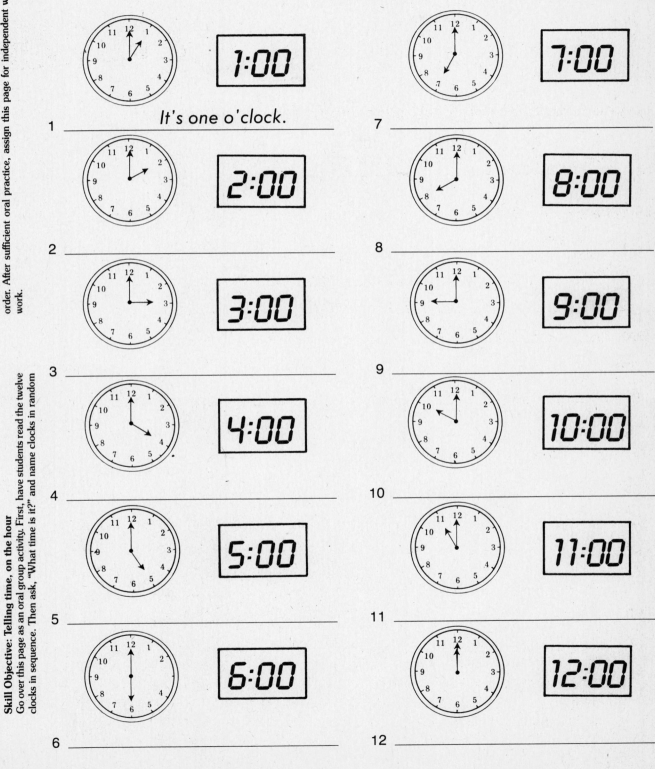

1   _____ It's one o'clock.

2   _____

3   _____

4   _____

5   _____

6   _____

7   _____

8   _____

9   _____

10 _____

11 _____

12 _____

Matching Times

Write the letter of the matching clock.

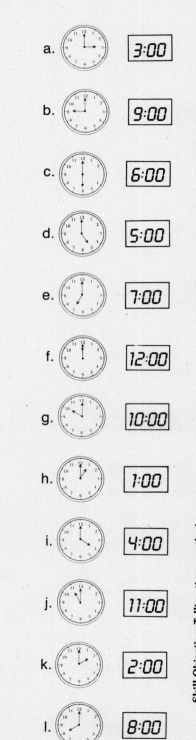

___c___ 1. It's six o'clock.

_____ 2. It's twelve o'clock.

_____ 3. It's three o'clock.

_____ 4. It's seven o'clock.

_____ 5. It's four o'clock.

_____ 6. It's nine o'clock.

_____ 7. It's five o'clock.

_____ 8. It's ten o'clock.

_____ 9. It's one o'clock.

_____ 10. It's two o'clock.

_____ 11. It's eleven o'clock.

_____ 12. It's eight o'clock.

a. 3:00

b. 9:00

c. 6:00

d. 5:00

e. 7:00

f. 12:00

g. 10:00

h. 1:00

i. 4:00

j. 11:00

k. 2:00

l. 8:00

Skill Objective: Telling time, on the hour
Draw attention to the clocks on the right side of the page. Name a clock by its letter, and ask a student to tell the time. Give all students a chance to respond at least once to the question, "What time is it?" For further practice, state a time ("It's ten o'clock.") and have students identify, by letter, the correct clock. After sufficient practice assign this page for independent work.

What Is It?

sure students understand the directions, then assign this page for independent written work.

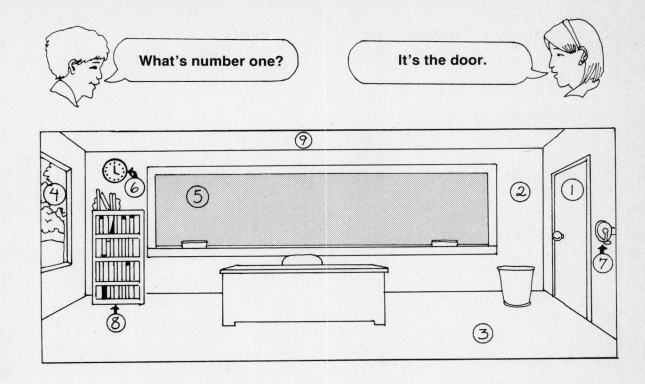

Find the number in the picture. Then write the sentence. The first one is done for you.

1. _It's the door._

2. _____

3. _____

4. _____

5. _____

6. _____

7. _____

8. _____

9. _____

Skill Objective: Naming classroom furniture and objects
Teach or review the vocabulary highlighted on this page. Have students use the picture to quiz each other: "What's number . . .?" "It's the (clock)." Make

---

MEMORY BANK

board	clock	door
floor	pencil sharpener	wall
ceiling	bookcase	window

The Days of the Week

Sunday	Monday	Tuesday	Wednesday	Thursday	Friday	Saturday
SUN S	MON M	TUES T	WED W	THURS T or TH	FRI F	SAT S

A. Write X in the box for the day.

		Sun	Mon	Tues	Wed	Thurs	Fri	Sat
1.	Tuesday			X				
2.	F							X
3.	Mon							
4.	W							
5.	Thurs							
6.	Sunday							
7.	Sat							
8.	M							
9.	Sun							
10.	Wed							

WHAT

DAY

IS

IT?

B. Answer the questions.

1. Is this Sunday?   *Yes, it's Sunday.*

2. Is this Friday?   *No, it's Wednesday.*

3. Is this Tuesday?   _____

4. Is this Saturday?   _____

5. Is this Monday?   _____

6. Is this Thursday?   _____

7. Is this Wednesday?   _____

Skill Objectives: Naming the days of the week, using a chart Teach or review the days of the week. If possible, let students examine several calendars and note the different abbreviations used. Point out that in the U.S., Sunday is considered the first day of the week. Ask students if this is true in their native countries. (Often, Monday is counted as the first of the week.) Do several examples from Parts A and B as a group, before assigning this page for independent work.

The Months of the Year

JANUARY						
S	M	T	W	T	F	S
1	2	3	4	5	6	7
8	9	10	11	12	13	14
15	16	17	18	19	20	21
22	23	24	25	26	27	28
29	30	31				

FEBRUARY						
S	M	T	W	T	F	S
			1	2	3	4
5	6	7	8	9	10	11
12	13	14	15	16	17	18
19	20	21	22	23	24	25
26	27	28	29			

MARCH						
S	M	T	W	T	F	S
				1	2	3
4	5	6	7	8	9	10
11	12	13	14	15	16	17
18	19	20	21	22	23	24
25	26	27	28	29	30	31

APRIL						
S	M	T	W	T	F	S
1	2	3	4	5	6	7
8	9	10	11	12	13	14
15	16	17	18	19	20	21
22	23	24	25	26	27	28
29	30					

MAY						
S	M	T	W	T	F	S
		1	2	3	4	5
6	7	8	9	10	11	12
13	14	15	16	17	18	19
20	21	22	23	24	25	26
27	28	29	30	31		

JUNE						
S	M	T	W	T	F	S
					1	2
3	4	5	6	7	8	9
10	11	12	13	14	15	16
17	18	19	20	21	22	23
24	25	26	27	28	29	30

JULY						
S	M	T	W	T	F	S
1	2	3	4	5	6	7
8	9	10	11	12	13	14
15	16	17	18	19	20	21
22	23	24	25	26	27	28
29	30	31				

AUGUST						
S	M	T	W	T	F	S
		1	2	3	4	
5	6	7	8	9	10	11
12	13	14	15	16	17	18
19	20	21	22	23	24	25
26	27	28	29	30	31	

SEPTEMBER						
S	M	T	W	T	F	S
						1
2	3	4	5	6	7	8
9	10	11	12	13	14	15
16	17	18	19	20	21	22
23	24	25	26	27	28	29
30						

OCTOBER						
S	M	T	W	T	F	S
	1	2	3	4	5	6
7	8	9	10	11	12	13
14	15	16	17	18	19	20
21	22	23	24	25	26	27
28	29	30	31			

NOVEMBER						
S	M	T	W	T	F	S
				1	2	3
4	5	6	7	8	9	10
11	12	13	14	15	16	17
18	19	20	21	22	23	24
25	26	27	28	29	30	

DECEMBER						
S	M	T	W	T	F	S
						1
2	3	4	5	6	7	8
9	10	11	12	13	14	15
16	17	18	19	20	21	22
23	24	25	26	27	28	29
30	31					

A.

1. April is before ___*May*___.

2. November is before _____.

3. July is before _____.

4. January is before _____.

5. September is before _____.

6. March is before _____.

B.

1. August is after ___*July*___.

2. February is after _____.

3. April is after _____.

4. December is after _____.

5. July is after _____.

6. October is after _____.

What's The Date?

January	February	March
JAN (the first month) 1	FEB (the second month) 2	MAR (the third month) 3
April	May	June
APR (the fourth month) 4	MAY (the fifth month) 5	JUN (the sixth month) 6
July	August	September
JUL (the seventh month) 7	AUG (the eighth month) 8	SEP or SEPT (the ninth month) 9
October	November	December
OCT (the tenth month) 10	NOV (the eleventh month) 11	DEC (the twelfth month) 12

Write the date.

1.
DECEMBER 1984
S M T W T F S
2 3 4 5 6 7 8
9 10 11 12 13 14 15
16 17 18 19 20 21 22
23 24 25 26 27 28 29
30 31

December 20, 1984 or _12/20/84_

2.
MARCH 1985
S M T W T F S
1 2
3 4 5 6 7 8 9
10 11 12 13 14 15 16
17 18 19 20 21 22 23
24 25 26 27 28 29 30
31

_____ or _____

3.
AUGUST 1985
S M T W T F S
1 2 3
4 5 6 7 8 9 10
11 12 13 14 15 16 17
18 19 20 21 22 23 24
25 26 27 28 29 30 31

_____ or _____

4.
SEPTEMBER 1984
S M T W T F S
1
2 3 4 5 6 7 8
9 10 11 12 13 14 15
16 17 18 19 20 21 22
23 24 25 26 27 28 29
30

_____ or _____

5.
APRIL 1985
S M T W T F S
1 2 3 4 5 6
7 8 9 10 11 12 13
14 15 16 17 18 19 20
21 22 23 24 25 26 27
28 29 30

_____ or _____

6.
NOVEMBER 1984
S M T W T F S
1 2 3
4 5 6 7 8 9 10
11 12 13 14 15 16 17
18 19 20 21 22 23 24
25 26 27 28 29 30

_____ or _____

7.
JANUARY 1985
S M T W T F S
1 2 3 4 5
6 7 8 9 10 11 12
13 14 15 16 17 18 19
20 21 22 23 24 25 26
27 28 29 30 31

_____ or _____

NOTE: You write: December 20   You say: "December twentieth"
You write: 1984   You say: "nineteen eighty-four"

Teach the number form of the date. Note that the first number refers to the month, the second refers to the day. Let students rewrite the dates on the board in this form. Ask students to read the dates on this page aloud, then assign as written work.

Skill Objectives: Reading a calendar, writing dates Teach ordinal numbers. Have students ask each other, "What's the (fifth) month?" Write the date on the board; demonstrate how it is read. Have students write their birthdates on the board; let others read the dates aloud.

What's The Matter?

I feel homesick.

I don't understand.

tired   angry   sad   sick   nervous

Write the sentences.

I don't understand.

I feel angry.

Skill Objective: Describing feelings
Teach or review the vocabulary highlighted on this page. Have the class mime the emotions illustrated at the top of the page. Each time ask: "What's the matter?" The class will respond: "We feel . . . ." Then encourage students to ask each other, "What's the matter?" and respond as they choose. Assign the page for independent written work.

May I?

A. Read these dialogues with a friend.

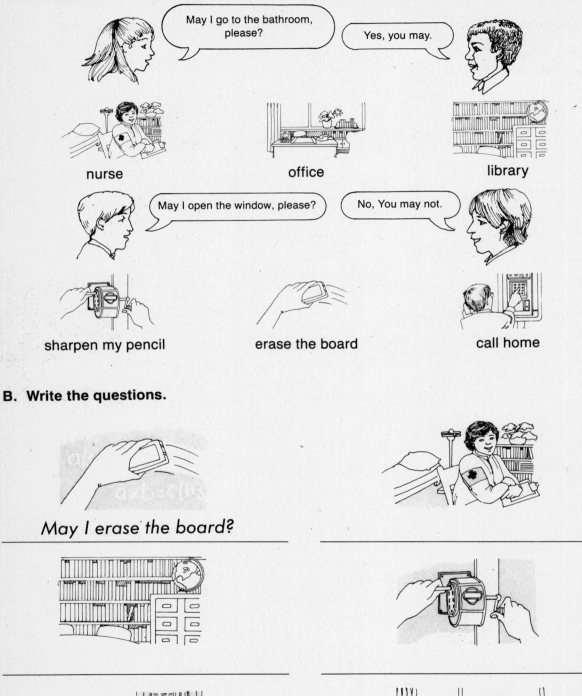

nurse

office

library

sharpen my pencil

erase the board

call home

restrict themselves to the places and actions pictured on this page. Be sure all students have a chance to participate in this oral practice. Assign the page for independent written work.

B. Write the questions.

May I erase the board?

Skill Objective: Asking permission
Teach or review the vocabulary on this page. Let students practice asking each other permission to go places and do things. They should use the forms: "May I . . . , please?" and "Yes, you may./No, you may not." Students need not

What's Your Name?

A. Answer the questions. Use complete sentences. The first one is done for you.

1. What is her first name?

   Her first name is Rita.

2. What is her last name?

   _____

3. Where is she from?

   _____

4. What is his first name?

   _____

5. What is his last name?

   _____

6. Where is he from?

   _____

My name is Rita Gonzales. I'm from Mexico.

My name is Dao Nguyen. I'm from Vietnam.

B. How about you? Answer these questions.

1. What is your first name?

   _____

2. What is your last name?

   _____

3. Where are you from?

   _____

4. What is your teacher's name?

   _____

Where is s(he) from?" Introduce yourself using the same structures and follow-up questions. Be sure to write your name on the board. Briefly review the questions in Part B orally, then assign the page for independent written work.

Skill Objective: Introducing oneself and others
Go over Part A orally with the class. Then encourage students to introduce themselves using the structures: "My name is . . . . I'm from . . . ." Check their classmates' understanding by asking: "What's her/his first (last) name?"

Names, Addresses, and Numbers

A. Answer the question.

1. What is his first name? _____

2. What is his last name? _____

3. What is his address?

_____

_____

4. What is his zip code? _____

5. What is his telephone number?

_____

B. Answer the question.

1. What is her first name? _____

2. What is her last name? _____

3. What is her address?

_____

_____

4. What is her zip code? _____

5. What is her telephone number?

_____

C. How About You? Answer these questions.

1. What is your name?

_____
    (first)   (last)

2. What is your address? Zip code?

_____

_____

3. What is your telephone number?

_____

Skill Objective: Giving mailing address and phone number. Teach or review the vocabulary used on these address forms. Demonstrate how zip codes and phone numbers are read. Practice reading the two labels with the class, then let volunteers dictate their addresses and phone numbers to their classmates. Write each address and phone number on the board, so that students can correct their writing. If you wish, have students answer the questions orally before assigning this page for independent work.

More Names, Addresses, and Numbers

A. Answer the questions. The first one is done for you.

1. Is his first name Peter? _Yes, it is._

2. Is his last name Smith? _____

3. What is his phone number? _____

4. Is his zip code 02117? _____

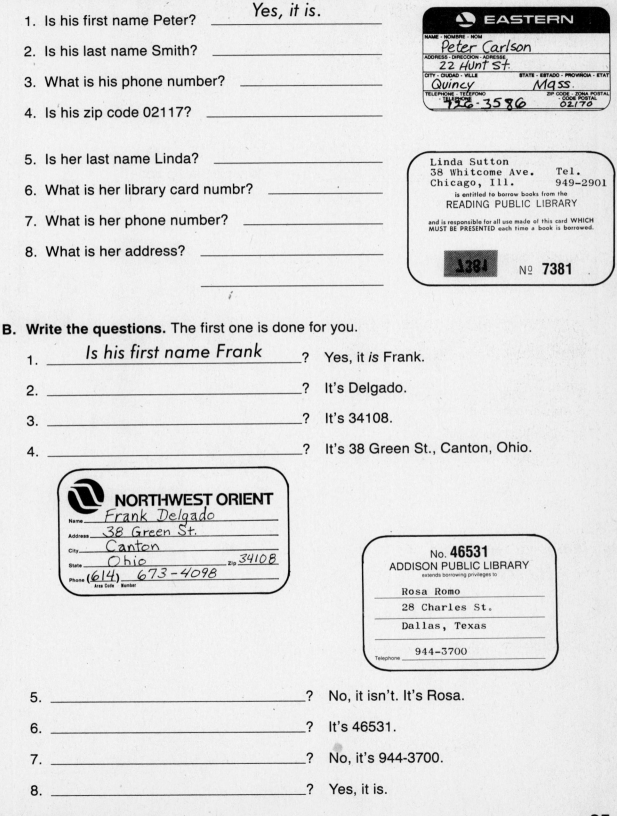

5. Is her last name Linda? _____

6. What is her library card numbr? _____

7. What is her phone number? _____

8. What is her address? _____

_____

B. Write the questions. The first one is done for you.

1. _____Is his first name Frank_____? Yes, it _is_ Frank.

2. _____? It's Delgado.

3. _____? It's 34108.

4. _____? It's 38 Green St., Canton, Ohio.

5. _____? No, it isn't. It's Rosa.

6. _____? It's 46531.

7. _____? No, it's 944-3700.

8. _____? Yes, it is.

What's His Name?

Hi! My name is Manuel Rodriguez. At school, I am Manuel. At home, my name is Manolo. With my friends, I am Papo. With my basketball coach, I am Rodriguez. At work, I am Manny. I am a boy with many names!

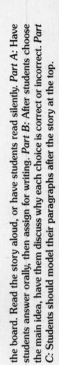

A. What is his name with:

1. his math teacher? _____

2. his mother? _____

3. his sister? _____

4. his friend Pablo? _____

5. his coach? _____

6. his principal? _____

7. his boss? _____

8. his father? _____

B. What is this story mostly about? Circle the best answer.

Manuel and his family.

Manuel and his teachers.

Manuel and his names.

Manuel and his friends.

C. Are you a person with more than one name, too? Write a paragraph like Manny's.

Hi! My name is _____

_____

_____

_____

_____

_____

_____

Skill Objectives: Identifying main ideas and details, writing a paragraph

Ask several students to give their full names and their nicknames ("What does your family call you? What do your friends call you?") List the nicknames on the board. Read the story aloud, or have students read silently. *Part A:* Have students answer orally, then assign for writing. *Part B:* After students choose the main idea, have them discuss why each choice is correct or incorrect. *Part C:* Students should model their paragraphs after the story at the top.

What's This?

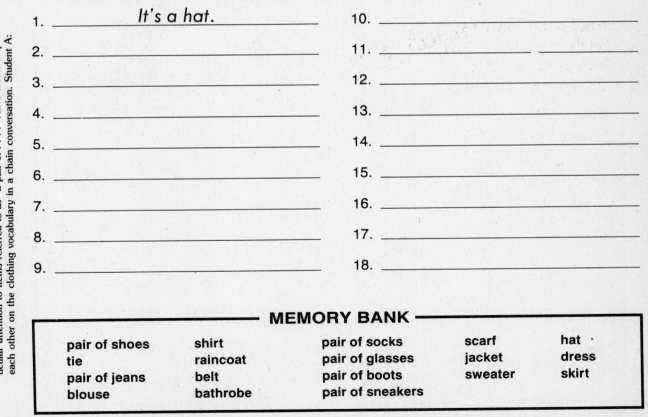

Find the picture. Write the sentence. The first one is done for you.

1. _It's a hat._
2. _____
3. _____
4. _____
5. _____
6. _____
7. _____
8. _____
9. _____

10. _____
11. _____
12. _____
13. _____
14. _____
15. _____
16. _____
17. _____
18. _____

── MEMORY BANK ──

pair of shoes	shirt	pair of socks	scarf	hat
tie	raincoat	pair of glasses	jacket	dress
pair of jeans	belt	pair of boots	sweater	skirt
blouse	bathrobe	pair of sneakers		

And What's This?

Write or complete the sentences. The first one is done for you.

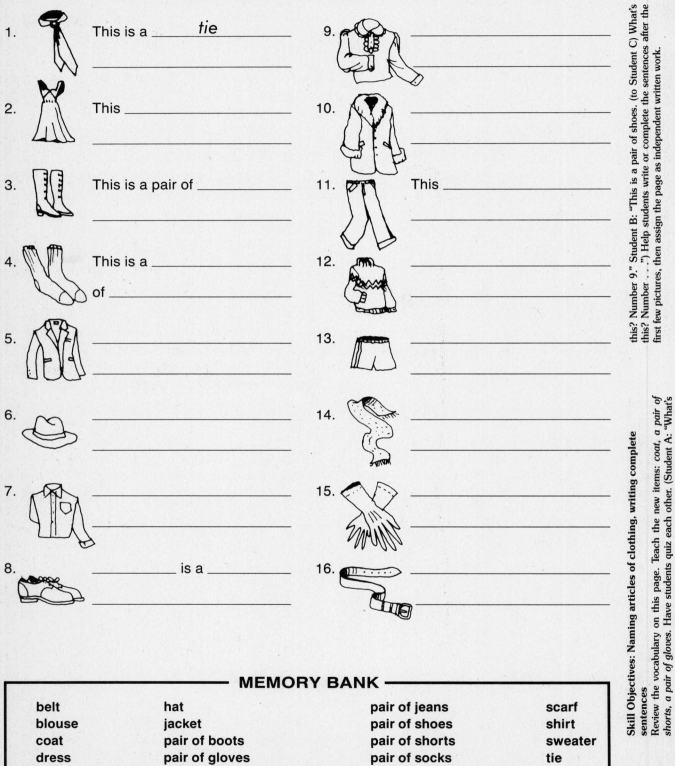

1. This is a _____tie_____ _____

2. This _____

3. This is a pair of _____

4. This is a _____ of

5. _____

6. _____

7. _____

8. _____ is a _____

9. _____

10. _____

11. This _____

12. _____

13. _____

14. _____

15. _____

16. _____

MEMORY BANK

belt	hat	pair of jeans	scarf
blouse	jacket	pair of shoes	shirt
coat	pair of boots	pair of shorts	sweater
dress	pair of gloves	pair of socks	tie

Skill Objectives: Naming articles of clothing, writing complete sentences

Review the vocabulary on this page. Teach the new items: *coat, a pair of shorts, a pair of gloves.* Have students quiz each other. (Student A: "What's this? Number 9." Student B: "This is a pair of shoes. (to Student C) What's this? Number . . .") Help students write or complete the sentences after the first few pictures, then assign the page as independent written work.

What Are They Wearing?

Write what each person is wearing. The first one is done for you.

1. *She is wearing a T-shirt and a pair of shorts.*

2. _____

3. _____

4. _____

5. _____

6. _____

7. _____

8. _____

Skill Objective: Discussing clothes
Review clothing vocabulary by making a statement about what you are wearing. ("I am wearing a blouse, a skirt and a sweater.") Ask students: "What are you wearing?" "What is (Maria) wearing?" Have students read the description written under the first picture. In each description, students should list two items the person is wearing. Have the class do all or some of this page orally before assigning as written work. Listen for correct use of the pronouns *she* and *he*.

Your Clothes

A. Study these size charts.

MEN
suits, coats, slacks (pants), jeans, jackets
32 34 36 38 40 42 44
(regular and long)
shoes, boots, slippers, sneakers
5 6 7 8 9 10 11 12 13
shirts
neck: 14 15 16 17
sleeve: 31 32 33 34 35 36
Small, Medium, Large

WOMEN
dresses, suits, skirts, blouses, slacks
6 8 10 12 14 16 18 20
junior sizes: 5 7 9 11 13
shoes, boots, slippers, sneakers
5 6 7 8 9 10
Small = sizes 6–10
Medium = sizes 12–14
Large = sizes 16–18

B. The tags tell you how to take care of your clothes. Read the tags, then read the sentences below. Write *yes* or *no* after each sentence.

MACHINE WASH LINE DRY

HAND WASH COOL WATER MADE IN U.S.A.

MACHINE WASH NO BLEACH TUMBLE DRY

DRY CLEAN ONLY MADE IN TAIWAN

YES OR NO?

1. Wash the pants in the washing machine. _____

2. Wash the sweater in the washing machine. _____

3. Wash the sweater in cool water. _____

4. Dry the pants in the dryer. _____

5. Wash the skirt in the washing machine. _____

6. Dry the skirt in the dryer. _____

7. Dry the shirt in the dryer. _____

8. The sweater and the skirt are made in Taiwan. _____

Skill Objective: Discussing clothing size and care
As a class, study the size charts at the top of the page. If you wish, ask students what shoe size they would buy here. What shoe size would they buy in their native land? Have students identify the clothes shown in Part B and read the labels. Explain and discuss all unfamiliar vocabulary. Have the class respond to Part B orally. When the response is "No," ask, "What do you have to do?" Assign the page as independent written work.

Odd Man Out

A. Odd Man Out. Circle the word that doesn't belong. The first one is done for you.

1. Bob, Paul, (Mary,) Dick
2. five, seven, first, ten
3. street, avenue, road, skirt
4. Monday, Thursday, Friday, March
5. red, yes, blue, yellow

6. blouse, shoes, boots, sandals
7. teacher, library, principal, nurse
8. wearing, looking, sitting, morning
9. she, they, his, I
10. brown, blouse, blue, pink

B. Write the questions. The first one is done for you.

What's your name?	Is his first name Tom?
What's her last name?	What's your favorite color?
What's this?	Who's wearing shorts?
Is this a tie?	How much are these boots?
What's she looking for?	Are these pajamas exchangeable?

1. _____*Is this a tie*_____? Yes, it is.
2. _____? It's red.
3. _____? They're $25.00
4. _____? My name is Ann.
5. _____? It's Taylor.
6. _____? She's looking for underwear.
7. _____? No, his first name is Joe.
8. _____? John is.
9. _____? Yes, they are.
10. _____? It's a sweater.

Skill Objectives: Classifying, asking/answering questions
Part A: Discuss the first example as a class. You may wish to let students work in pairs on this section, then discuss and correct as a class. *Part B:* Have students note that the questions are provided in the box. They are to write the appropriate question in front of each answer. Do some or all of these items orally before assigning the page as independent or pair work.

Money! Money! Money!

A. How much is it worth? Write the words.

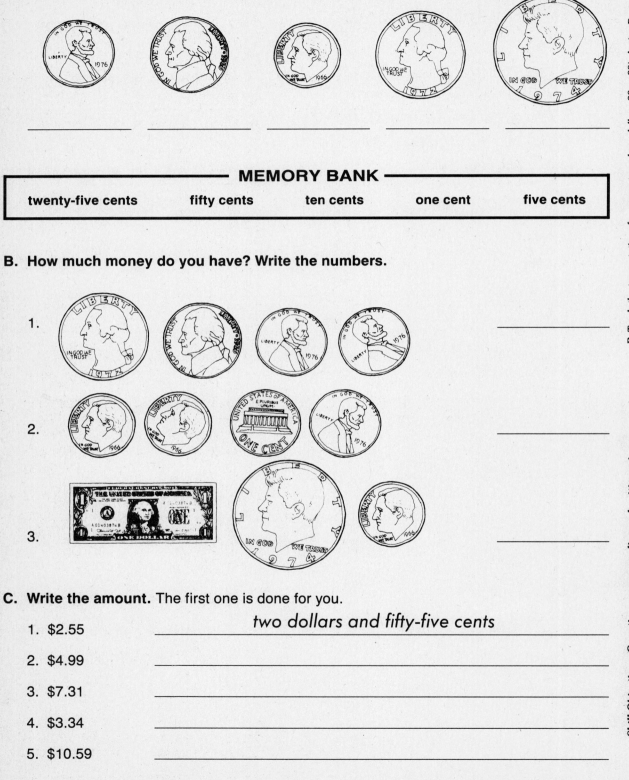

_____ _____ _____ _____ _____

MEMORY BANK

| twenty-five cents | fifty cents | ten cents | one cent | five cents |

B. How much money do you have? Write the numbers.

1. _____

2. _____

3. _____

C. Write the amount. The first one is done for you.

1. $2.55   *two dollars and fifty-five cents*

2. $4.99   _____

3. $7.31   _____

4. $3.34   _____

5. $10.59 _____

Skill Objectives: Counting money, reading and writing prices Bring coins and bills to class. Have students practice counting money, reporting and writing each amount as a number and a phrase. *Part A:* Have the class identify the value of each coin, then let students write the answers. *Part B:* Teach the two notations for amounts under a dollar: .39 or 39¢. Assign Part B, then correct and discuss as a class. *Part C:* Have students read the prices aloud. Note that $2.55 is read as "two fifty-five," but written as *two dollars and fifty-five cents.*

Buying Clothes

A. Practice this conversation with a classmate.

- How much is the **skirt** on sale?
- It's **$20.**
- What is the regular price of the **skirt**?
- It's **$25.**
- How much do you save?
- You save **$5.**

Now ask and answer the same questions about all the clothes on sale.

B. Work with a classmate. Complete this conversation any way you like.

- How much is this . . .?
- It's . . .
- Is it on sale?

- Yes, ...
  No, ...

- Can I return it?

- Yes, ...
  No, ...

- I'll take it!
- Cash or charge?
- . . . .
- Thank you!

Sale Today!

MAIN STREET CLOTHING
Save 10% to 20%

SALE : $20.00
REGULAR: $25.00

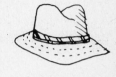

SALE: $12.00
REGULAR $15.00

SALE: $8.00
REGULAR: $10.00

SALE : $13.00
REGULAR : $18.00

SALE : $10.00
REGULAR: $11.00

SALE : $18.00
REGULAR: $20.00

SALE: $55.00
REGULAR: $60.00

SALE: $40.00
REGULAR: $45.00

SALE: $24.00
REGULAR: $48.00

SALE: $5.00
REGULAR: $7.00

Money Problems

Answer these questions.

1. Ben has a penny, two dimes, three nickels, and a quarter. *How much* money is this?

   _____

2. Mary is buying a scarf. It is eight dollars and fifty cents. She has a ten dollar bill. How much is Mary's *change*?

   _____

3. A shoe store is having a sale. Mrs. Yakos is buying two pairs of sneakers. How much money is that?

   _____

4. Look at the sweater, the pair of jeans, and the pair of boots. Willie has a twenty dollar bill.

   Can he buy the sweater, jeans, and boots? _____

   Can he buy the sweater and the jeans? _____

   Can he buy the sweater? _____

   How much is his change? _____

5. This is the Baxter family. They are eating chicken dinners. *Each* dinner is $5.00. How much is the bill?

   _____

6. James and June are *twins.* It's their birthday today. Their father and mother are giving them $30.00. The twins are *dividing* the money *evenly.* How much is June's present?

   _____

Skill Objectives: Understanding math language and money transactions
Bring in real coins and bills, or use realistic "play money." Put price tags on classroom objects. Let students roleplay salesperson and customer: selecting items, computing the bill, deciding if it is affordable, paying and receiving change. Supervise closely, or allow independent pair practice, depending on the skill level of your group. Discuss the page to decide which math process must be used to solve each problem, then assign for independent work.

Missing Words

Skill Objective: Recognizing and completing familiar phrases
On this page, students use context clues to complete simple sentences and dia-
logues. Do several examples as a class. Draw attention to the fact that a number of different responses can be correct. Example: "What color/size is his
shirt?" "Is this/that your hat?" Have students complete the page independently, then discuss their answers as a class.

A. Write in a word to complete the sentence. The first one is done for you.

1. Tom is _____*wearing*_____ a green jacket.

2. What _____ is his shirt?

3. Is _____ your hat?

4. Mary isn't wearing a _____ dress.

5. Fred and Paul _____ friends.

6. This is _____ friend.

7. _____ is wearing a yellow sweater?

8. Is _____ name Peter?

B. Fill in the missing words.

1. —Is this your umbrella?

    —No, ____*that*____ is my umbrella.

2. —Who _____ wearing blue jeans?

    —Bob _____.

3. —What's _____?

    —It's a bathrobe.

4. —What is Sally _____?

    —She's _____ a white blouse.

5. —Is _____ coat black?

    —No, _____ is blue.

6. —Is _____ friend wearing a coat?

    —No, _____ isn't.

Frannie

Frannie is going to a party. She is wearing her favorite clothes. She is wearing a white blouse. Her skirt is gray. She's wearing her favorite black shoes. Her sweater is blue.

It is cold tonight. Frannie is wearing her brown coat and her blue hat. She is very pretty!

A. Answer the following questions. Use short answers. The first one is done for you.

1. Where is Frannie going? _____ *to a party* _____

2. What color is her blouse? _____

3. What color is her skirt? _____

4. What color are her shoes? _____

5. What color is her sweater? _____

6. What color is her hat? _____

7. Why is Frannie wearing her coat? _____

B. What is this story mostly about? Circle the best answer.

a. Frannie and her clothes

b. Frannie and a party

c. Frannie and her blouse

d. Frannie and her friends

C. What about you? Fill in the blanks for your clothes. Then answer the questions.

1. What color __*are*__ your __*shoes*__ ? *They are* _____

2. What color _____ your _____ ? _____

3. What color _____ your _____ ? _____

4. What color _____ your _____ ? _____

5. What color _____ your _____ ? _____

Skill Objectives: Identifying main idea and details, using pronouns Ask students color questions: "What color is/are your . . . (shoes, eyes, hair, book)?" Have students use pronoun replacements in answering: "They're brown." "It's blue." Read the story aloud. Part A: Students may answer questions orally before writing. Part B: After students have chosen the main idea, have them discuss why each choice is correct or incorrect. Part C: Do some examples as a group, then assign for independent work. Students should use pronouns in their answers.

What Time Is It?

Write the sentence. The first two are done for you.

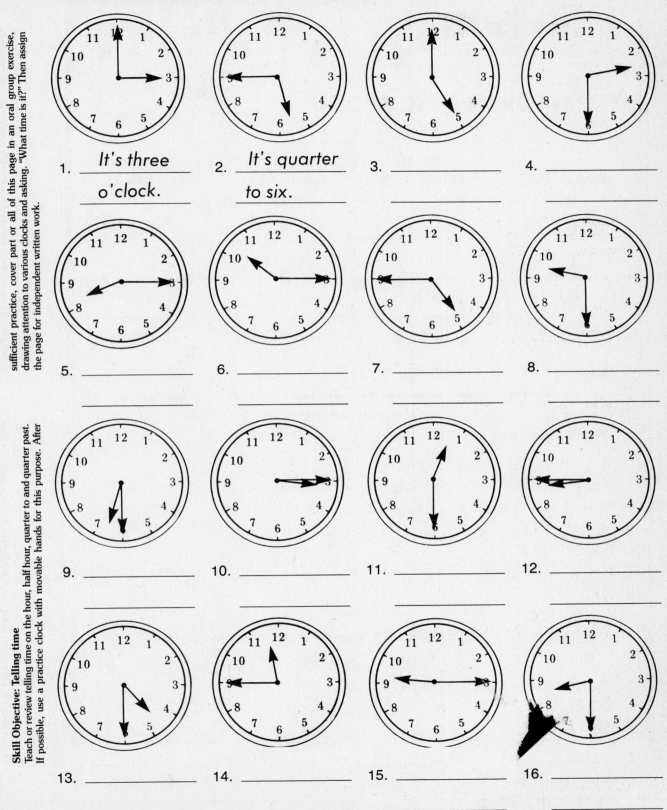

sufficient practice, cover part or all of this page in an oral group exercise, drawing attention to various clocks and asking "What time is it?" Then assign the page for independent written work.

Skill Objective: Telling time
Teach or review telling time on the hour, half hour, quarter to and quarter past. After. If possible, use a practice clock with movable hands for this purpose.

1. _It's three o'clock._

2. _It's quarter to six._

3. _____

4. _____

5. _____

6. _____

7. _____

8. _____

9. _____

10. _____

11. _____

12. _____

13. _____

14. _____

15. _____

16. _____

Bus Schedule

Hudson BUS COMPANY

Daily Service

YORKTOWN -- BOXFORD

One way - **$ 5.00**
Round trip - **$ 9.50**

DEPARTING	TIME OF DEPARTURE	ARRIVING	TIME OF ARRIVAL
YORKTOWN	6:00 a.m.	BOXFORD	8:00 a.m.
BOXFORD	8:30 a.m.	YORKTOWN	10:30 a.m.
YORKTOWN	11:00 a.m.	BOXFORD	1:00 p.m.
BOXFORD	1:30 p.m.	YORKTOWN	3:30 p.m.
YORKTOWN	4:00 p.m.	BOXFORD	6:00 p.m.

Circle the correct answer to complete each sentence. The first one is done for you.

1. The first bus from Yorktown: Departing time is . . . .
   a. 11:00 a.m.   b. 4:00 p.m.   c. 6:00 a.m.

2. The bus trip from Yorktown to Boxford is . . . .
   a. two hours   b. one hour   c. three hours

3. The first bus from Boxford to Yorktown is at . . . .
   a. 1:30 p.m.   b. 8:30 a.m.   c. 6:00 a.m.

4. There are . . . morning bus trips to Boxford.
   a. one   b. two   c. three

5. The price of a one-way ticket from Boxford to Yorktown is . . . .
   a. $5.00   b. $10.00   c. $15.00

6. The last bus to Yorktown: Departing time is . . . .
   a. 6:00   b. 4:00   c. 1:30

MEMORY BANK

round trip	one way	departing (leaving)
a.m. (morning)	arriving (coming)	p.m. (afternoon)

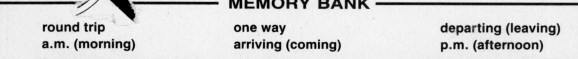

Skill Objective: Reading a chart
Teach/review vocabulary on the bus schedule. Ask questions about bus times and ticket prices. Help students examine the schedule to find answers. When students are comfortable with this chart reading skill, direct attention to the multiple choice questions under the chart. Have students read the first example aloud, inserting the three alternative endings. Students must check the bus schedule to discover which answer is correct. Do another example together, then assign for independent work.

Where Are They?

Write *in*, *on*, *under* or *behind*.

1. The jacket is _____ the slacks.

2. The bathrobe is _____ the closet.

3. The nightgown is _____ the bed.

4. The jeans are _____ the shirt.

5. The socks are _____ the shoes.

6. The blouse is _____ the chair.

7. The woman is _____ the table.

8. The table is _____ the floor.

9. The scarf is _____ the door.

10. The shoes are _____ the window.

Where Are My Things?

Write in the answers. The first one is done for you.

1. **Where are my shoes?** — _They're under the bed._

2. **Where is my notebook?** — _____

3. **Where is my green tie?** — _____

4. **Where are my books?** — _____

5. **Where are our jackets?** — _____

6. **Where is my belt?** — _____

7. **Where are my keys?** — _____

Skill Objective: Using prepositions: *in, on, under, behind, in front of, behind Luis.*") To structure *under,* have the student hold a book over his/her head. Cover part or all of this page orally before assigning as independent written work. Students are to draw their own picture cue before answering the last question.

Write the highlighted prepositions on the board. Ask one student to sit on his/her desk. Have students answer the question: "Where is (Angela)?" in different ways as you point to each preposition. ("She's in the classroom/on her desk/

Maps

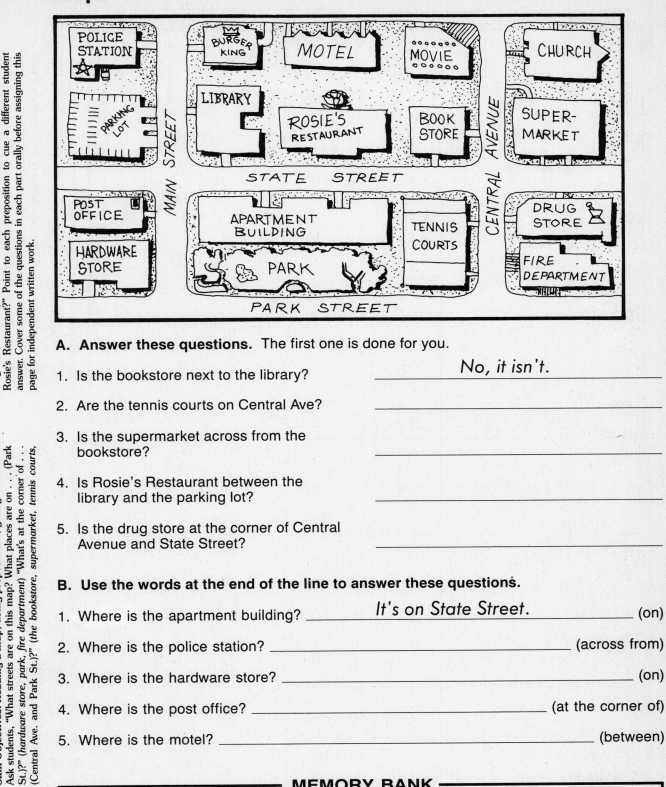

drugstore) List the phrases: *on, next to, between, across from.* Ask, "Where's Rosie's Restaurant?" Point to each preposition to cue a different student answer. Cover some of the questions in each part orally before assigning this page for independent written work.

Skill Objectives: Reading a map, using prepositions, giving directions Ask students, "What streets are on this map? What places are on . . . (Park St.)?" (*hardware store, park, fire department*) "What's at the corner of . . . (Central Ave. and Park St.)?" (*the bookstore, supermarket, tennis courts,*

A. Answer these questions. The first one is done for you.

1. Is the bookstore next to the library? _____No, it isn't._____

2. Are the tennis courts on Central Ave? _____

3. Is the supermarket across from the bookstore? _____

4. Is Rosie's Restaurant between the library and the parking lot? _____

5. Is the drug store at the corner of Central Avenue and State Street? _____

B. Use the words at the end of the line to answer these questions.

1. Where is the apartment building? _____It's on State Street._____ (on)

2. Where is the police station? _____ (across from)

3. Where is the hardware store? _____ (on)

4. Where is the post office? _____ (at the corner of)

5. Where is the motel? _____ (between)

── MEMORY BANK ──

at the corner of	across from	next to	on	between

Following Directions

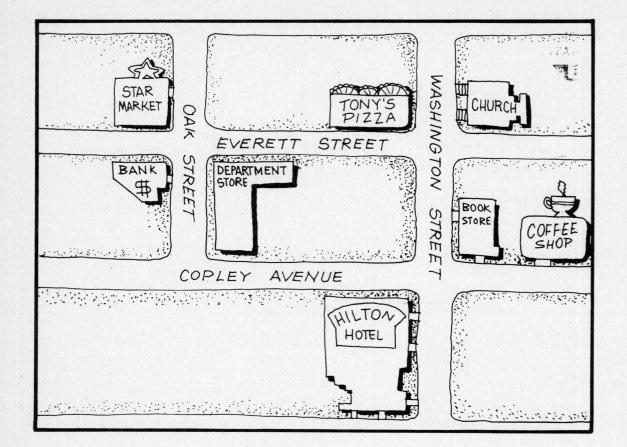

Skill Objectives: Reading a map, following directions
Write the following phrases on the board: *on*, *at the corn·r of*, *next to*, *across from*. Ask volunteers to use these phrases to orally describe the location of each place on the map. Go over the instructions to this page. Complete the first few items as a class, comparing and correcting each drawing. Then assign the page as independent or pair work.

Read the sentences below. Draw the places on the map. Write the names of the places.

1. The *hospital* is on Copley Avenue next to the Hilton Hotel.
2. The *high school* is at the corner of Washington St. and Everett St., across from Tony's Pizza.
3. The *park* is on Copley Avenue across from the coffee shop.
4. The *music store* is at the corner of Oak St. and Everett St.
5. The *beauty shop* is between the music store and Tony's Pizza.
6. *Gary's Gas Station* is on Everett St., across from the church.
7. *Sam's Sandwich Shop* is on Oak Street next to Star Market.
8. The *parking lot* is next to the hospital.
9. A *telephone booth* is next to the bank on Everett Street.
10. The *playground* is on Everett Street next to the church.
11. The *office building* is across from the beauty shop on Everett St.
12. The *bus station* is across from the Hilton Hotel, next to the high school.

The Surprise Party

Today is Mario's birthday. His mother is giving him a surprise party. His new friends Ramon and Thomas are in the living room. They are behind the sofa. Maria is under the table. Antonio is in the closet behind the coats.

Carlos, Robert, and Nancy are behind the chairs. Mrs. Mendez is in the kitchen. Mario's brothers and sisters are behind the kitchen door. Everyone is waiting for Mario. They want to yell "Surprise!"

A. Answer the following questions. The first one is done for you.

1. What day is today? *It is Mario's birthday.* _____

2. Where are Ramon and Thomas? _____

    _____

3. Who is under the table? _____

4. Where are Carlos, Robert, and Nancy? _____

    _____

5. Where are Mario's brothers and sisters? _____

    _____

6. What does everyone want to yell? _____

B. What is this story mostly about? Circle the best answer.

a. Mario's new friends

b. Mario's surprise party

c. Mario's happy family

d. Mario's mother

C. Write the name of each person in the place where he or she is hiding. Be sure to include all Mario's friends, his brothers and sisters, and his mother.

Anna Garcia

A. Circle the best word. The first one is done for you.

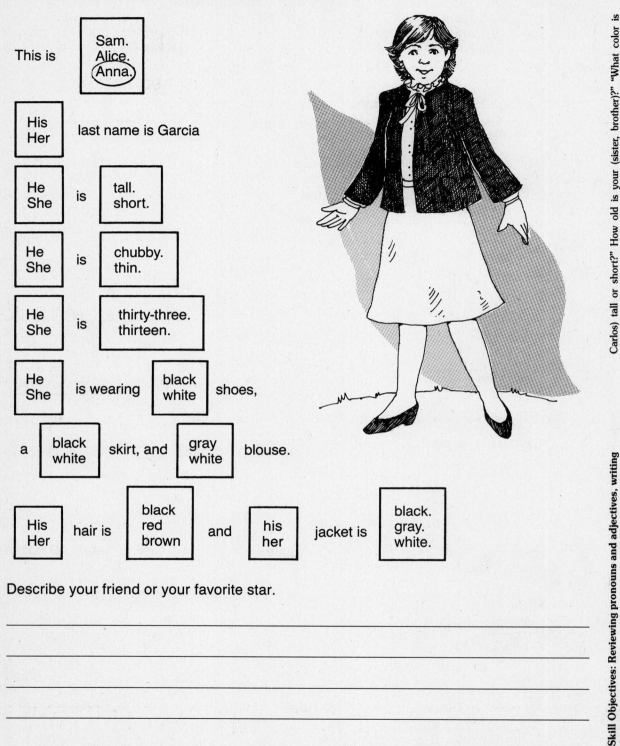

This is | Sam. Alice. (Anna.)

His / Her | last name is Garcia

He / She | is | tall. / short.

He / She | is | chubby. / thin.

He / She | is | thirty-three. / thirteen.

He / She | is wearing | black / white | shoes,

a | black / white | skirt, and | gray / white | blouse.

His / Her | hair is | black red brown | and | his / her | jacket is | black. gray. white.

B. Describe your friend or your favorite star.

_____

_____

_____

_____

_____

_____

Skill Objectives: **Reviewing pronouns and adjectives, writing descriptions**

Briefly review the pronouns *he, she, his, her* by asking students questions about their classmates: "What is (Anna's, Mario's) last name?" "Is (Laura, Carlos) tall or short?" How old is your (sister, brother)?" "What color is (Manuel's) hair?" Do Part A as an oral group exercise before assigning as independent written work. Explain that students can use Part A as a model as they write their own descriptive paragraph in Part B.

Describing People and Things

Write the sentences. Use the adjectives in the Memory Bank. The first two are done for you.

TED   JAN

1.

84   14

a. _____*Ted is old.*_____

b. _____*Jan is young.*_____

LINDA   GINA

2.

a. _____

b. _____

JOSE   CARLOS

3.

a. _____

b. _____

SOFIA   AGATHA

4.

a. _____

b. _____

5.

$100,000.00 $20.00

a. _____

b. _____

6.

a. _____

b. _____

MEMORY BANK

thin	short	cheap	fat
expensive	big	small	beautiful
young	old	tall	ugly

The Verb "To Be"

A. Fill in the missing words. The first one is done for you.

I am (I'm)	She is (She's)	We are (We're)	They are (They're)
He is (He's)	It is (It's)	You are (You're)	

Hello. I ___am___ Ying Yee. I _____ from China. ·

This is my class. We _____ from different countries.

She _____ Maria. She _____ from Greece.

He _____ Amin. He _____ from Lebanon.

They _____ Luis and Rosa. They _____ from Mexico.

B. Write about these students. The first one is done for you.

Jose
Puerto Rico

He is Jose.
He is from
Puerto Rico.
_____
_____

Claudette
France

_____
_____
_____
_____
_____

Samir   Gina
Syria

_____
_____
_____
_____

You

_____

C. Read parts A and B again. Then answer these questions.

Is Maria from Greece? _____   Is Ying Yee from China? _____

Is Amin from Greece? _____   Are Luis and Rosa from Mexico? _____

Is Claudette from Puerto Rico? _____   Are you from Mexico? _____

Are Samir and Gina from France? _____   Is your teacher from China? _____

Where is Maria from? _____   Where is Amin from? _____

Where are you from? _____   Where are Samir and Gina from? _____

Skill Objective: Reviewing present forms of "to be" Ask students, "Where are you from? Where is (Paco, Verjik) from? Where are Gina and Tomas from? Where is (Paco, Verjik) from? Where are you and Ari from?" Use the responses to build a chart on the board with the present forms of "to be." Review the chart together. Do Part A as an oral exercise before assigning as independent work. Discuss the first examples in Part B and C as a class, then assign the page for independent writing.

Using the Verb "To Be"

pendent work. *Part B:* Explain the directions, then do the exercise as an oral group practice before assigning as independent work.

A. Write the correct word in the blank space. The first one is done for you.

1. John _____*is*_____ in class today.

2. Linda and Janet _____ sisters.

3. I _____ tired today.

4. The weather today _____ beautiful.

5. Sharon _____ a cashier.

6. She and I _____ cousins.

7. My English book _____ easy.

8. Henry and Fred _____ sick today.

9. You _____ from New York.

10. They _____ good friends.

Skill Objectives: Reviewing present forms of "to be," constructing questions and negative statements

Go over some or all of Part A as an oral group review before assigning as inde-

B. Write a question. Write a negative answer.

1. Pam is a student.　　(Question)　*Is Pam a student?*

　　　　　　　　　　　(Negative)　*No, Pam is not a student.*

2. It is ten o'clock.　　(Question)　_____

　　　　　　　　　　　(Negative)　_____

3. Susan is from New York.　(Question)　_____

　　　　　　　　　　　(Negative)　_____

4. Mary and Amy are sick today.　(Question)　_____

　　　　　　　　　　　(Negative)　_____

5. The books are on the desk.　(Question)　_____

　　　　　　　　　　　(Negative)　_____

6. Mr. Jones is in the office.　(Question)　_____

　　　　　　　　　　　(Negative)　_____

Writing About People

A. Read these paragraphs. Fill in the missing words.

1. This is Akira Katogi. His native country is Japan. His native language is Japanese. His address in the United States is:

   43 Exeter Lane
   Denver, Colorado 80267

2. This is Angela Leone. Her native _____

   is Italy. _____ native language

   _____ Italian. Her _____ in the

   _____ States is:

   3317 Keystone Avenue
   Los Angeles, California 90024

B. How about you?

My name _____

_____

_____

_____

_____

_____

C. Write about a classmate.

_____

_____

_____

_____

_____

_____

Skill Objectives: Completing familiar phrases, writing paragraphs *Part A:* Read the first description with the class. Have students ask each other questions based on the text. Write their questions on the board: "What's his name? What's his native country?" etc. *Part B:* Students will use the description. *Part C:* Students will interview a partner and write a paragraph based on this information. If they wish, students can refer to the questions written on the board.

Dream Dates

A. Read the sentences. Write the letter of the matching picture.

a   b   c   d   e

1. My dream date is tall. He has dark hair and dark eyes.

   He is fifteen years old. _____

2. My dream date is short. She is chubby and pretty, too.

   She is thirteen. _____

3. My dream date is thin. He is short, and his hair is

   blond. He is wearing a hat. _____

4. My dream date is tall. I am short, but I want a tall

   girl friend. She is wearing a bathing suit. _____

B. Write about your dream date.

_____

_____

_____

C. Interview a classmate. What is her/his dream date like?

_____

_____

_____

Skill Objectives: Describing, asking questions, writing a paragraph
Ask one student to think of a classmate. The other students will ask questions to discover who that person is. Provide structure by asking questions yourself: "Is it a boy? Is he tall? Does he have brown eyes? Is he wearing . . .?" Play several rounds of the game, then ask volunteers to describe the people pictured on this page. After students have completed Part A, they can compare answers. Remind students to use complete sentences as they write the descriptions in Parts B and C.

Letters to a Friend

Dear Rosanna,
This is a picture of my boyfriend, Manuel. He's tall and thin and he's very handsome! His hair is black, and in this picture he's wearing a sweater and jeans.
Your friend,
Lisa

Dear Ben,
This is my new girlfriend. Her first name is Julia, her last name is Garcia. She is a Mexican American. Her mother is from Texas, and her father is from Acapulco. She's short. She's 14 and very friendly and pretty.
Your friend,
Carlos

Write a letter to a friend. Draw a picture of a boyfriend or girl friend you want—a real person or a star.

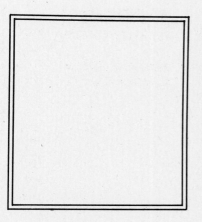

Skill Objectives: Describing, writing a friendly letter Ask volunteers to read the two letters aloud. Have students note the placement and form of the greeting and closing, and the indention of the first line of the letter. Have students suggest questions to ask the letter writers: "What's your (boy)friend's name? What does he look like? How old is he?" Let other students answer. After drawing a picture, students will write a letter describing their friend. The letters at the top of the page will serve as models for form and content.

Dear Dot

Skill Objectives: Reading comprehension, making judgments
Draw attention to the title of the page. Ask students where they have read sim-
ilar advice columns. Read the letter aloud. Explain any unfamiliar words. Ask
students to reread the letter silently, then answer questions 1-5. Correct these

answers and let students compare their choice of advice. Read Dot's answer
together. Clarify the word *infatuated* and other new vocabulary. Let students
agree or disagree with Dot's reply and perhaps offer some other solutions.

Dear Dot—

I'm fifteen and I'm in love. He is tall and handsome. He has black hair and big, brown eyes. He is
wearing a nice blue suit today. I am sitting right in
front of him. He is writing on the board. I love to
look at him, and that is my problem—he is my history teacher. What can I do?

Lovesick

1. Is her "boyfriend" short? _____

_____

2. What color are his hair and eyes? _____

_____

3. What's he wearing today? _____

_____

4. Who is this "boyfriend"? _____

_____

5. What is your advice for Lovesick? Draw a line under your answer.

   a. Marry your teacher.

   b. Find a boyfriend your own age.

   c. Go to a new school.

   d. Change history teachers.

6. Now read Dot's answer. See if your answer is the same. If your answer is different, tell
   why you disagree. Dot's advice is below.

Dear Lovesick—

You are not in love, you are only infatuated.
How old is your teacher? He is too old for you. Stop
looking at him and look at the boys in your class.
You need a boy your own age.

Dot

Shopping for Food

A. Mr. Karlson is in the supermarket. What is he buying? Write the words. The first one is done for you.

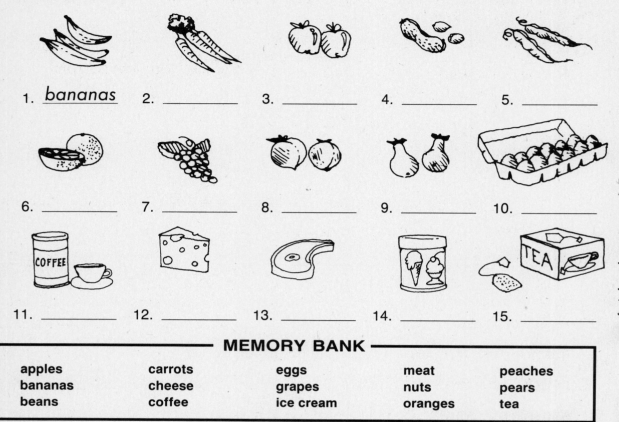

1. _bananas_   2. _____   3. _____   4. _____   5. _____

6. _____   7. _____   8. _____   9. _____   10. _____

11. _____   12. _____   13. _____   14. _____   15. _____

MEMORY BANK

apples	carrots	eggs	meat	peaches
bananas	cheese	grapes	nuts	pears
beans	coffee	ice cream	oranges	tea

B. Mrs. Harris is at home. Help her write a shopping list.

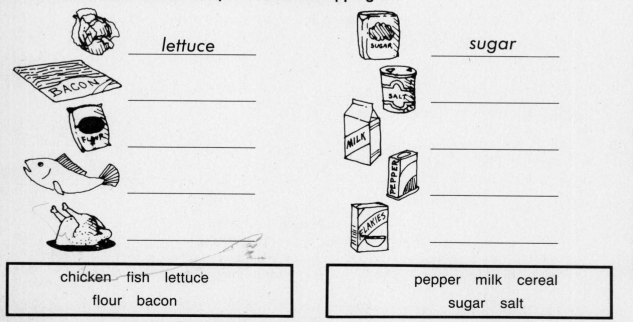

lettuce _____

_____

_____

_____

_____

sugar _____

_____

_____

_____

_____

chicken   fish   lettuce
flour   bacon

pepper   milk   cereal
sugar   salt

page for independent written work. For more practice with this skill, have the class decide upon a breakfast, lunch, or dinner menu, then draw up a shopping list for the meal.

Skill Objective: Recognizing count and mass nouns
Part A: Introduce or review the vocabulary. Point out the plural forms used for items 1-10, and the mass singular forms used for items 11-15. Do Part B as an oral group exercise. All the items in Part B are mass nouns. Assign the

Food! Food! Food!

Read the question. Look at the picture. Then write the answer.
The first one is done for you.

written work. Listen carefully for correct use of count and mass nouns. (*Carrots* and *eggs* are the only nouns on this page using the plural form.)

Skill Objectives: Recognizing count and mass nouns, present progressive tense
Go over this page as an oral group activity before assigning for independent

1. What is she buying?

   She's buying carrots.

2. What is he buying?

3. What is she eating?

4. What is he eating?

5. What is the cat eating?

6. What is he drinking?

7. What is the cat drinking?

8. What is she drinking?

9. What is he cooking?

10. What is she cooking?

B The Burger House

Regular hamburger.	.59	Filet fish sandwich	.95
Regular cheeseburger	.69	Fried chicken sandwich . . .	.95
Double hamburger	1.15		
with cheese.	1.25	Regular coffee	.45
		Large coffee.	.65
Regular fries	.55	Milk.	.45
Large fries	.75	Reg. cola	.45
		Large cola	.65
Vanilla milk shake	.69	Reg. orange.	.45
Chocolate shake	.69	Large orange	.65
Strawberry shake.	.69	Reg. diet cola	.45
		Large diet cola	.65

A. Add up these bills. Are they correct?

Yes or No?

1. A regular hamburger, a regular French fries, and a regular cola is $1.59. _____

2. A double hamburger with a regular coffee is $1.49. _____

3. A fish sandwich, a large fries, and a regular diet cola is $2.15. _____

4. Two cheeseburgers, a large fries, and a large orange is $2.78. _____

5. A fried chicken sandwich and a strawberry milk shake is $1.64. _____

6. A double cheeseburger, a fish sandwich, a chocolate shake, and a large cola is $3.45. _____

B. Practice this conversation with a classmate.

—Can I help you?

—Yes, _____, please.

—Anything to drink?

— _____

—That's $_____ .

—Thank you.

Skill Objectives: Practicing money skills, using a chart. Discuss the menu with the class, then ask a student to place his/her order. "Can I help you?" "Yes, (a hamburger and large fries, please.)" "Anything to drink?" "Yes, a vanilla milk shake." Write the student's order on the board.

Have the class find the price of each item, then calculate the total bill. Repeat this activity several times. Do some examples as a class before assigning Part A for independent work. Part B: Allow plenty of time for students to practice the roleplay.

What's for Lunch?

Look at the picture. Find the matching word. Write the letter on the line. The first one is done for you.

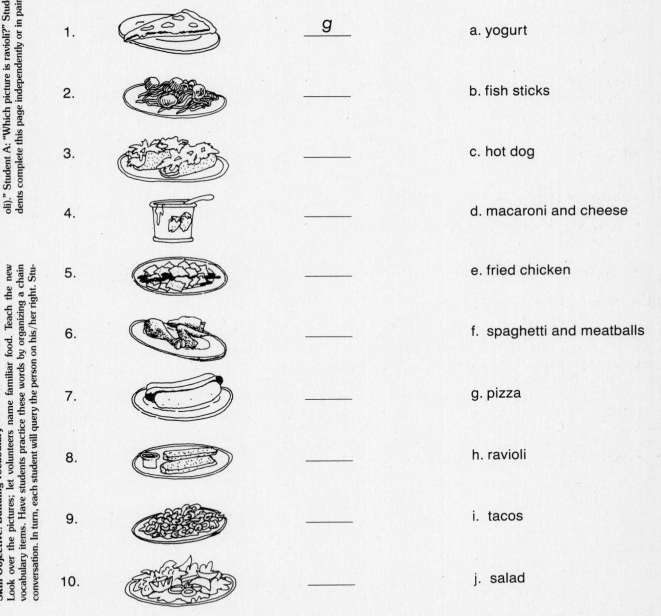

1. _____g_____   a. yogurt

2. _____   b. fish sticks

3. _____   c. hot dog

4. _____   d. macaroni and cheese

5. _____   e. fried chicken

6. _____   f. spaghetti and meatballs

7. _____   g. pizza

8. _____   h. ravioli

9. _____   i. tacos

10. _____   j. salad

More Food

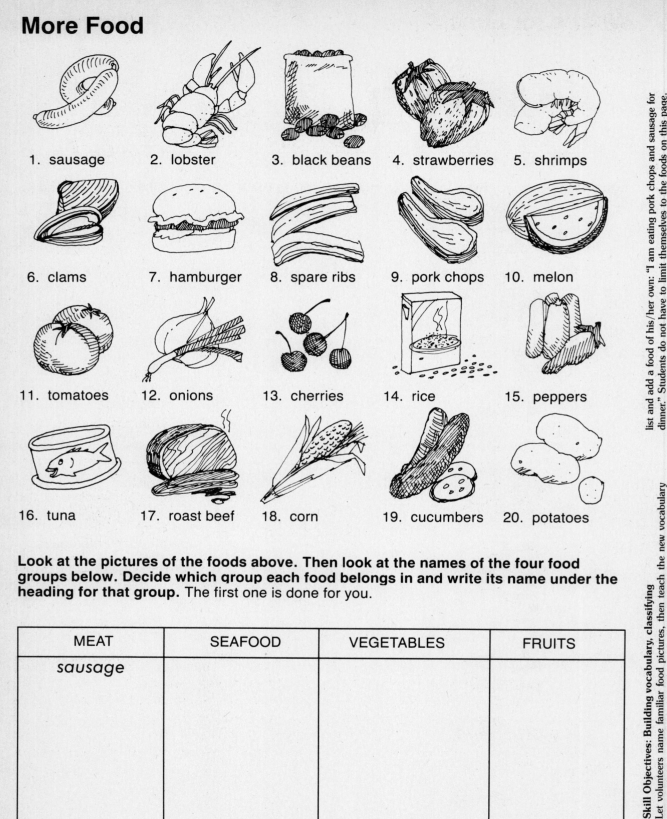

1. sausage
2. lobster
3. black beans
4. strawberries
5. shrimps
6. clams
7. hamburger
8. spare ribs
9. pork chops
10. melon
11. tomatoes
12. onions
13. cherries
14. rice
15. peppers
16. tuna
17. roast beef
18. corn
19. cucumbers
20. potatoes

Look at the pictures of the foods above. Then look at the names of the four food groups below. Decide which group each food belongs in and write its name under the heading for that group. The first one is done for you.

MEAT	SEAFOOD	VEGETABLES	FRUITS
sausage			

Skill Objectives: Building vocabulary, classifying Let volunteers name familiar food pictures, then teach the new vocabulary items. Play a cumulative list game for vocabulary reinforcement. Student A will say: "I am eating (pork chops) for dinner." The next student will repeat that list and add a food of his/her own: "I am eating pork chops and sausage for dinner." Students do not have to limit themselves to the foods on this page. Classify the first few foods as a group, then let students complete the lists independently.

What's She Buying?

Write the words. The first one is done for you.

that are packed in cans, boxes, or bags, or sold by the pound or quart. Teach/ review the vocabulary on this page. Let students quiz each other: "What's she buying? Number (5)." "She's buying a . . . ." After sufficient practice, assign for independent work.

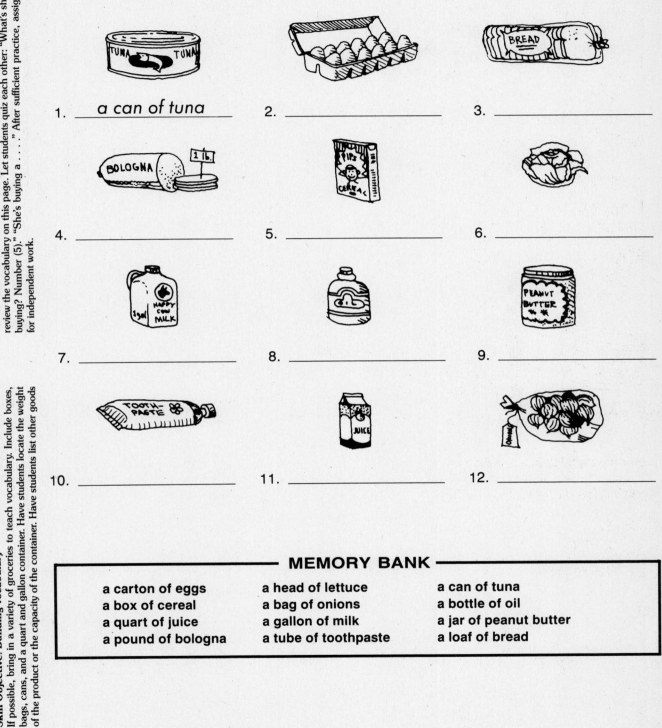

1. _a can of tuna_

2. _____

3. _____

4. _____

5. _____

6. _____

7. _____

8. _____

9. _____

10. _____

11. _____

12. _____

Skill Objective: Building vocabulary If possible, bring in a variety of groceries to teach vocabulary. Include boxes, bags, cans, and a quart and gallon container. Have students locate the weight of the product or the capacity of the container. Have students list other goods

---

MEMORY BANK

a carton of eggs	a head of lettuce	a can of tuna
a box of cereal	a bag of onions	a bottle of oil
a quart of juice	a gallon of milk	a jar of peanut butter
a pound of bologna	a tube of toothpaste	a loaf of bread

Odd Man Out

A. Odd Man Out: Circle the word that does not belong. The first one is done for you.

1. hamburger, (lettuce,) sausage, roast beef.
2. large, small, medium, first.
3. coffee, fish, milk, lemonade.
4. picture, drug store, school, restaurant.
5. near, across, is, in.
6. bed, table, shoe, chair.
7. eggs, box, can, jar.
8. second, three o'clock, ten thirty, quarter of one.
9. tall, old, fat, man
10. bacon, eggs, toast, ice cream.

B. Write the name of each item.

1. _____ *a can of tuna* _____

2. _____

3. _____

4. _____

5. _____

6. _____

7. _____

8. _____

9. _____

10. _____

Skill Objectives: Reviewing food vocabulary, classifying *Part A:* Odd Man Out is a classification activity. Do the first few examples as a group, then assign for independent work. Correct as a class. Ask students to explain why their choice does not belong. *Part B:* Assign for independent work, or if you prefer, review first as an oral group exercise.

A or An?

A. When is it _A_, and when is it _AN_?

Use AN before a vowel (a, e, i, o, u) or a vowel sound:
  an apple   an egg   an hour   an honest man

Use A before a consonant, or a consonant-sounding vowel:
  a banana   a used car   a teacher   a sandwich

B. Fill in with _A_ or _AN_. Then practice reading the sentences aloud with a friend.

1. He is reading _____ *an* _____ English book.

2. Lisa is _____ pretty girl.

3. Tom is eating _____ apple.

4. Mrs. Thompson is _____ old woman.

5. Maria is buying _____ banana and _____ pear.

6. James is studying at _____ university in New York.

7. Luis is eating _____ orange.

8. Mrs. Lee is wearing _____ red dress.

9. My father is _____ honest man.

10. She is eating _____ egg for breakfast.

11. Paul is looking at _____ new car.

12. David is _____ thin boy.

13. The baby is eating _____ ice cream cone.

14. The boy is buying _____ umbrella.

15. Sandra is wearing _____ orange coat.

16. Michael is wearing _____ blue shirt.

17. Sally is _____ eight year old girl.

18. Mr. Jones is _____ happy man.

19. The boy is eating _____ carrot.

20. Jack is sitting on _____ chair.

article *a* is used before words beginning with long *u*: *a used car*. Practice the examples and other words orally before assigning Part B for independent and pair work.

Skill Objective: Using articles *a* and *an*
Go over the article rules on the top of this page with the class. Point out that *an* is used in words beginning with a silent *h*: *an hour, an honest man*. The

Dear Dot

Dear Dot—

My mother is on a diet. My sister is on a diet. My grandmother is on a diet. I am NOT on a diet, and there is nothing good to eat in my house. I like steak and pork chops, potatoes and rice. I want an ice cream or a pizza <u>NOW</u>! My mother is eating only salad and fish. My sister is eating only carrots, cucumbers, and tomatoes. My grandmother is eating only chicken and lettuce. I am STARVING! What can I do?

A Hungry Boy

1. Who is on a diet? _____

_____

2. What does the boy like? _____

_____

3. What is his mother eating? _____

_____

4. What is his sister eating? _____

_____

5. What is his grandmother eating?

_____

6. What is your advice for Hungry Boy? Circle your answer.

   a. Go on a diet too.   c. Go to a restaurant to eat every night.

   b. Eat only candy; don't eat at home.   d. Eat diet meals at home and other food outside.

7. Now read Dot's answer. See if your answer is the same. If your answer is different, tell why you disagree. Dot's advice is below.

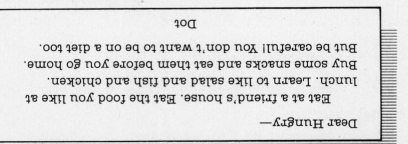

Dear Hungry—

Eat at a friend's house. Eat the food you like at lunch. Learn to like salad and fish and chicken. Buy some snacks and eat them before you go home. But be careful! You don't want to be on a diet too.

Dot

Skill Objectives: Reading comprehension, making judgments
Have students recall the previous "Dear Dot" page. Read the letter aloud as students follow along. Explain any unfamiliar words. Ask students to reread the letter silently, then answer questions 1-6. Correct the first five answers, then let students compare their choice of advice. Read Dot's answer together. Let students tell why they agree or disagree with Dot's reply and perhaps offer some other solutions.

Where Are You From? What Do You Do?

Look at the pictures and answer these questions:

What nationality are you?
Where are you from?
What's your occupation?

The first two are done for you.

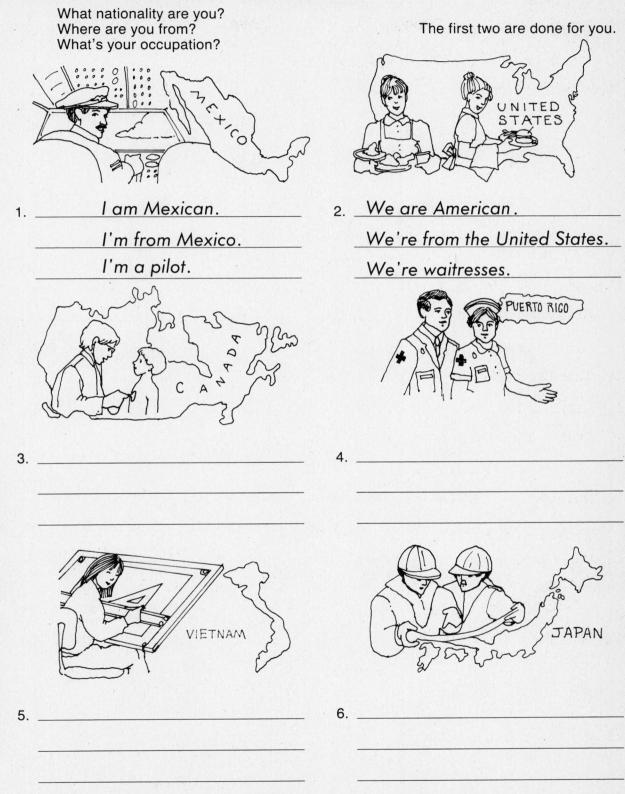

1. *I am Mexican.*
   I'm from Mexico.
   I'm a pilot.

2. *We are American.*
   We're from the United States.
   We're waitresses.

3. _____

4. _____

5. _____

6. _____

Where Are They From? What Do They Do?

Look at the pictures and answer these questions:

What nationality is he or she, or what nationality are they?
Where is he or she from, or where are they from?
What's his or her occupation, or what's their occupation?

The first one is done for you.

1. _He is Cuban._

   He's from Cuba.

   He's an accountant.

2. _____

   _____

   _____

3. _____

   _____

   _____

4. _____

   _____

   _____

5. _____

   _____

   _____

6. _____

   _____

   _____

Skill Objective: Discussing nationalities and occupations
This is an extension of page 61. Have students recall information they learned about their classmates. Ask: "Where are Amin and Anna from? What nationality is Kostas?" etc. Teach/review the occupations shown on this page. Do some or all of the exercises as an oral group activity. Listen for the correct pronoun and verb form. Assign for independent written work.

More Occupations

A.
Find the hidden words.

1. dressmaker
2. mechanic
3. taxi driver
4. chef
5. builder
6. painter
7. teacher
8. pilot
9. nurse
10. singer
11. musician
12. actor

```
s  a  d  r  e  s  m  e  s  t  a
f  o  r  e  c  i  l  w  o  a  r
o  r  e  c  h  e  r  l  a  x  i
d  a  s  m  e  c  h  a  n  i  c
r  i  s  e  c  r  e  l  i  d  e
a  t  m  b  u  i  l  d  e  r  b
t  e  a  c  h  e  r  e  s  i  u
e  h  k  a  i  p  a  i  n  v  i
m  f  e  r  e  a  l  c  h  e  f
i  a  r  p  a  i  n  t  e  r  m
p  c  a  r  s  t  u  n  k  e  r
i  t  c  t  o  r  r  u  r  s  e
l  o  r  a  s  i  s  p  i  l  o
o  r  s  i  n  g  e  r  m  e  s
t  a  r  m  u  s  i  c  i  a  n
```

B. Circle the best answer.

1. Is your father a cook?

    a. Yes, he is.
    b. He's singing.
    c. He's cooking now.

2. What is your sister's job?

    a. She's single.
    b. Yes, she is.
    c. She's a cashier.

3. Is your brother studying English?

    a. He's a sales clerk.
    b. No, he isn't.
    c. He's from Brazil.

4. Where is Ali from?

    a. He's from Egypt.
    b. He's studying now.
    c. He's a mechanic.

5. Is your sister married?

    a. No, he isn't.
    b. No, she's single.
    c. She's a dressmaker.

Skill Objectives: Discussing occupations, building vocabulary
Review the occupations listed in Part A through an oral riddle game. Give clues such as the following: "She is fixing the bus. What is she? (a mechanic) He is driving the family to the airport. What is he? (a taxi driver)" If appropriate, let students offer riddles of their own. To prepare for Part B, ask students parallel questions: "What is your sister's job? Is your brother married? Where is (Samir) from?" Assign the page as independent work.

OCCUPATION	10,000	15,000	20,000	25,000	30,000	35,000	40,000	45,000	50,000	55,000	60,000	65,000	70,000	75,000	80,000
Chef	▓	▓	▓												
Pilot	▓	▓	▓	▓	▓	▓	▓								
Rock star	▓	▓	▓	▓	▓	▓	▓	▓	▓	▓	▓	▓	▓	▓	▓ →
Doctor	▓	▓	▓	▓	▓	▓	▓	▓	▓	▓	▓				
Engineer	▓	▓	▓	▓	▓	▓	▓								
Teacher	▓	▓													
Astronaut	▓	▓	▓	▓	▓	▓	▓								

Salary Graph

A. Read the sentences below carefully and fill in the blanks.

1. I'm an engineer. My salary is $ _____45,000_____ a year.

2. I'm a pilot. My salary is $ _____ a year.

3. I'm a doctor. My salary is $ _____ a year.

4. I'm an astronaut. My salary is $ _____ a year.

5. I'm a teacher. My salary is $ _____ a year.

6. I'm a chef. My salary is $ _____ a year.

7. I'm a rock star. My salary is more than $ _____ a year.

B. Read these sentences. Answer with *YES* or *NO*.

1. A teacher's salary is more than a chef's.   _____

2. A doctor's salary is $65,000 a year.   _____

3. An astronaut's salary and a doctor's salary are the same.   _____

4. An engineer's salary is less than a teacher's.   _____

5. A rock star's salary is more than $80,000 a year.   _____

6. A chef's salary is $25,000 a year.   _____

Skill Objectives: Reading a bar graph, understanding *more than, less than*. Examine the graph with the class. For each occupation, ask: "What is the . . .'s salary?" Teach the phrases and concepts *more than* and *less than*. Ask: "Which salaries are more than/less than the (pilot's) salary?" After sufficient practice, have students work independently. Correct and discuss the page as a class. If appropriate, have students research other professional salaries and, as a class, draw up their own salary bar graph.

Interviewing

A. Interview people in your school. Ask these questions. Write their answers in the chart.

What's your name?   What do you want to be?

How old are you?   What's your favorite color?

What's your nationality?   What's your favorite food?

Name	Age	Nationality	Occupation	Favorite Color	Favorite Food

B. Write a paragraph about some of the people above.

_____

_____

_____

_____

_____

_____

_____

Dear Dot

Dear Dot—

    This is my problem. I want to be an actor, but my father says, "No!" I want to take drama classes next year. My father says, "Take computer programming." I don't want to go to college. My father says, "Go to college. Get an education." My father is not a college graduate, so it is important to him. But I want to act, not study. What can I do?

                      Hamlet

1. What does Hamlet want to be? _____

   _____

2. What classes does he want to take? _____

   _____

3. What does his father want him to take? _____

   _____

4. Is his father a college graduate? _____

   _____

5. What is your advice for Hamlet? Circle your answer.

   a. Do what your father says.

   b. Do what you want to do.

   c. Take both classes if possible.

   d. Leave home.

6. Now read Dot's answer. See if your answer is the same. If your answer is different, tell why you disagree. Dot's advice is below.

Dear Hamlet—

    Listen to your father. Take computer programming and drama. Today you want to be an actor. Tomorrow you may want to be an accountant. Remember, most actors go to college nowadays. The more you know, the better off you are. Good luck.

                      Dot

Skill Objectives: Reading comprehension, making judgments Have students recall the problems presented on previous "Dear Dot" pages. Read the letter aloud as students follow along. Explain unfamiliar words. Be sure students understand why the boy has signed his letter, "Hamlet." Ask the students to reread the letter then answer questions 1-5. Correct the first four answers, then let students compare their choice of advice. Read Dot's answer. Let students tell why they agree or disagree with Dot, and offer some other solutions.

Families

This is the Pilla family.

This is Mario Pilla and Gloria Pilla.

Mario and Gloria are married.
Mario is Gloria's husband.
Gloria is Mario's wife.
Mario and Gloria are parents.
Richard and Rose are their children.

This is Richard. He is their son.

This is Rose. She is their daughter.

Skill Objectives: Building vocabulary, asking/answering questions Teach/review the vocabulary on this page. Read the story about the Pilla family aloud. Ask questions about the text, then encourage students to ask each other questions following your models. "Are Gloria and Richard married? Who is the husband? Is Rose the daughter?" Do some of the questions as an oral group exercise, then assign the page as independent work. Remind students to answer the questions in Part B with complete sentences.

A. Check the right answer. The first one is done for you.

	YES	NO
1. Is Mario married?	✓	
2. Is Mario the wife?		
3. Is Gloria the daughter?		
4. Is Richard married?		
5. Is Richard the son?		
6. Is Rose the daughter?		
7. Are Mario and Gloria the children?		
8. Are Richard and Gloria the children?		
9. Are Richard and Rose the children?		
10. Are Mario and Gloria the parents?		

B. Answer the questions.

1. Who is the husband? _____

2. Who is his wife? _____

3. Who is the son? _____

4. Who is the daughter? _____

5. Who are the parents? _____

6. Who are the children? _____

MEMORY BANK

family	married	husband	wife
parents	son	daughter	children

Tom's Family

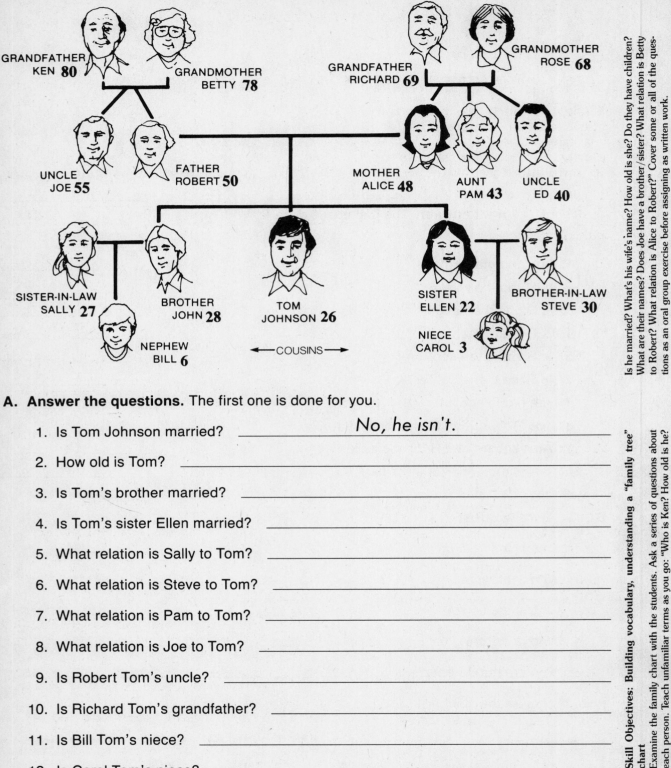

Is he married? What's his wife's name? How old is she? Do they have children? What are their names? Does Joe have a brother/sister? What relation is Betty to Robert? What relation is Alice to Robert?" Cover some or all of the questions as an oral group exercise before assigning as written work.

A. Answer the questions. The first one is done for you.

1. Is Tom Johnson married? _____ *No, he isn't.* _____

2. How old is Tom? _____

3. Is Tom's brother married? _____

4. Is Tom's sister Ellen married? _____

5. What relation is Sally to Tom? _____

6. What relation is Steve to Tom? _____

7. What relation is Pam to Tom? _____

8. What relation is Joe to Tom? _____

9. Is Robert Tom's uncle? _____

10. Is Richard Tom's grandfather? _____

11. Is Bill Tom's niece? _____

12. Is Carol Tom's niece? _____

13. What is Carol's relation to Bill? _____

Skill Objectives: Building vocabulary, understanding a "family tree" chart
Examine the family chart with the students. Ask a series of questions about each person. Teach unfamiliar terms as you go: "Who is Ken? How old is he?

Where Are They?

A. Answer the questions. The first one is done for you.

should answer with a negative contraction, then give the correct information using a pronoun contraction. ("No, they aren't. They're on the desk.") Encourage students to ask each other questions. Work orally, then assign the page for independent work.

1. Are you in the bedroom?

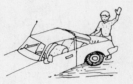

No, I'm not.

I'm in the kitchen.

_____

2. Is the cat in the yard?

_____

_____

3. Is Cathy on her bike?

_____

_____

4. Is Tom under the car?

_____

_____

B. Write the questions.

Skill Objectives: Forming contractions, reviewing prepositions
Set classroom objects on a desk. Example: a stack of different colored books, an eraser behind the books, a box with pencils in front of the books. Ask questions beginning, "Is/Are . . .?" ("Are the books under the desk?") Students

1. _____

_____

No, they aren't.

They're in the bathtub.

2. _____

_____

No, we aren't.

We're in front of the fireplace.

3. _____

_____

No, he isn't.

He's behind the tree.

4. _____

No, they aren't.

They're under the bed.

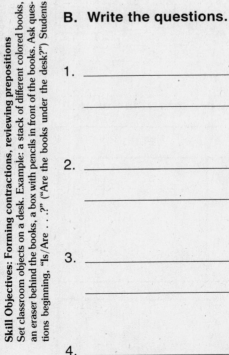

Bill's Apartment Building

A. Write the answer. Use *on* or *in*.

1. Where is the lobby?

   It's on the first floor.

2. Where is the laundry room?

   _____

3. Where is Bill's apartment?

   _____

4. Where is Bill's bedroom?

   _____

5. Where is the T.V. antenna?

   _____

6. Where is the store room?

   _____

7. Where is the elevator?

   _____

8. Where is Mrs. Doe's apartment?

   _____

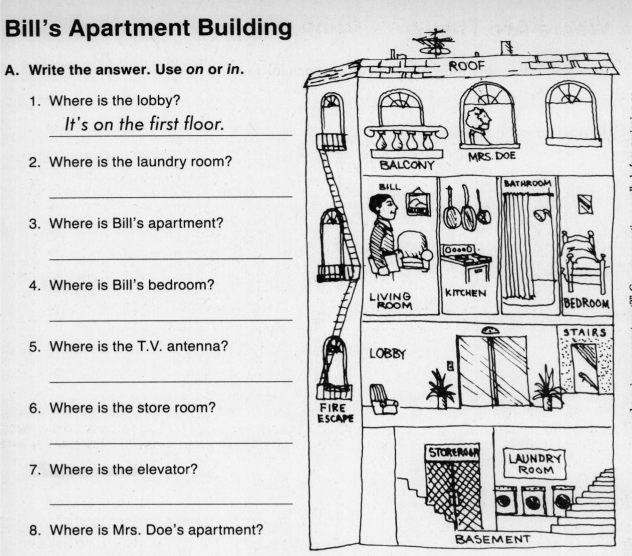

Skill Objectives: Building vocabulary, classifying you have in your apartment?" Go over questions orally before assigning as *Part A:* Discuss the apartment building. Ask "What is on the first floor? Where written work. *Part B:* Teach/review the vocabulary in the Memory Bank. Cat- is the laundry room?" etc. Listen for correct use of *in* and *on.* Ask students: "Do egorize the first few items as a group, then assign as independent work. you live in an apartment building? What floor do you live on? What rooms do

B. What is in each room? Fill in the chart. You may write each word more than once.

Living room	Kitchen	Bedroom	Bathroom

MEMORY BANK

armchair	dresser	rug	stove
bathtub	lamp	shower	table
bed	mirror	sink	toilet
chair	refrigerator	sofa	TV

The Green Family at Home

Here are some questions about the Green family. There are three answers after each question. Read all three answers. Decide which is the best answer and draw a line around it. The first one is done for you.

1. Where is Mr. Green?
   a. He's in the garage.   (b. He's in the kitchen.)   c. He's in the yard.

2. What is he doing?
   a. He's cooking dinner.   b. He's lying down.   c. He's eating dinner.

3. Where is Susie?
   a. She's in the garage.   b. She's in the living room.   c. She's in her bedroom.

4. What is she doing?
   a. She's reading a book.   b. She's playing records.   c. She's getting dressed.

5. Where is Bobby?
   a. He's in the bathroom.   b. He's in the garage.   c. He's in the living room.

6. What is he doing?
   a. He's cooking breakfast.   b. He's eating dinner.   c. He's taking a bath.

7. Where is Mrs. Green?
   a. She's in the living room. b. She's in the dining room.   c. She's in the yard.

8. What is she doing?
   a. She's listening to records. b. She's cooking lunch.   c. She's reading a book.

9. Where are the pets?
   a. They're in the yard.   b. They're in the garage.   c. They're in the kitchen.

10. What are they doing?
    a. They're eating.   b. They're taking a bath.   c. They're lying down.

The Ruiz Family

Hello! My name is Carmen Ruiz. I'm 15. I'm from Mexico. I am a student, and I'm in the tenth grade. My hair is long and black. I'm wearing blue slacks and my new red blouse.

My brother Luis is 24. He's an accountant. He's in his room. He's listening to music.

My father is a taxi driver. He is tall and thin. His hair is black. He's sitting on the sofa. He's reading a book.

My mother is a chef. She's in the kitchen. Her name is Rita. She's eating a sandwich.

A. Read each sentence. Write T if the sentence is true. Write F if it is false.
The first one is done for you.

1. The girl's name is Carmen Ruiz. _____ *T*

2. She is from Puerto Rico. _____

3. She is a chef. _____

4. Her hair is black. _____

5. Luis is her uncle. _____

6. He is 24. _____

7. He is reading a book. _____

8. Her father is short and chubby. _____

9. He is sitting on the sofa. _____

10. The girl's mother is drinking coffee. _____

B. Answer the questions. Use complete sentences. The first two are done for you.

1. Is the girl 15? _____*Yes, she is 15.*_____

2. Is she wearing black jeans? _____*No, she is wearing blue slacks.*_____

3. Is Luis an architect? _____

4. Is her father listening to music? _____

5. Is her mother a chef? _____

6. Is her mother in the living room? _____

7. Is her mother's name Rita? _____

8. Is her mother eating ice cream? _____

Skill Objectives: Present progressive, noting details, using contractions
Read the story aloud as students follow along. Ask yes/no questions about the text. Have students answer in complete sentences. If the answer is "no," students should supply the correct information. ("Is the girl's name Maria Ruiz?" "No, it's Carmen Ruiz." "Is Carmen wearing slacks and a blouse?" "Yes, she is.") Encourage students to ask each other questions using this structure. Do several examples together, then assign the page as independent work.

Dear Dot

Skill Objectives: Reading comprehension, making judgments
Read the letter aloud as students follow along. Explain any unfamiliar words.
Ask students to reread the letter silently, then answer questions 1–4. Correct
the first three answers, then let students compare their choice of advice. Read
Dot's answer together. Let students tell why they agree or disagree with Dot's
reply, and perhaps offer some other suggestions.

Dear Dot—

I am a girl with long, dark hair and dark eyes, and so is my sister. My favorite color is blue, and so is my sister's. We are both tennis players. We are twins! We are happy being twins, but here is our problem. Boys don't know who is who, so they don't ask us out. They feel nervous and silly because they can't tell us apart. I'm staying home too many Friday nights, and so is my sister. What can we do?

Lonely Twin

1. How are the sisters alike? _____

_____

_____

2. What is their problem? _____

_____

3. Why do the boys feel nervous and silly? _____

_____

4. What is your advice for Lonely Twin? Circle your answer.
   a. Be different from your sister.
   b. Call up boys and ask them for dates.
   c. Wear a name tag.
   d. Go out alone on Friday nights.

5. Now read Dot's answer. See if your answer is the same. If your answer is different, tell why you disagree. Dot's advice is below.

Dear Lonely Twin—

You and your sister are too much alike. Change your hair style. Wear different colors. Play different sports. If that doesn't work, wear name tags!

Dot

What Are They Doing?

A. Write the word under each picture.

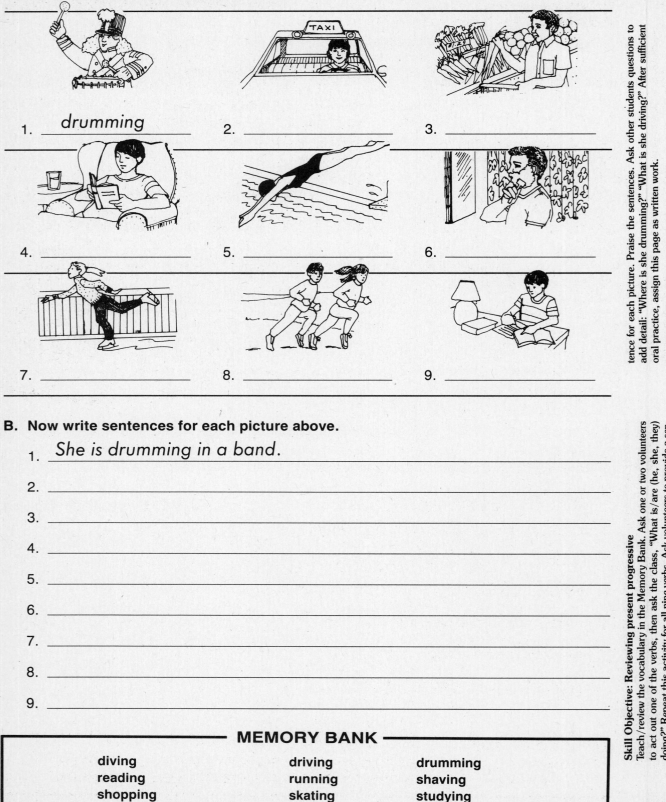

1. *drumming*

2. _____

3. _____

4. _____

5. _____

6. _____

7. _____

8. _____

9. _____

B. Now write sentences for each picture above.

1. *She is drumming in a band.*

2. _____

3. _____

4. _____

5. _____

6. _____

7. _____

8. _____

9. _____

┌─────────────────── **MEMORY BANK** ───────────────────┐

diving	driving	drumming
reading	running	shaving
shopping	skating	studying

└──┘

Skill Objective: Reviewing present progressive
Teach/review the vocabulary in the Memory Bank. Ask one or two volunteers to act out one of the verbs, then ask the class, "What is/are (he, she, they) doing?" Repeat this activity for all nine verbs. Ask volunteers to provide a sentence for each picture. Praise the sentences. Ask other students questions to add detail: "Where is she drumming?" "What is she driving?" After sufficient oral practice, assign this page as written work.

What's Happening at School Today?

Read the sentences carefully. Then write the number of the sentence next to the picture it describes. The first one is done for you.

1. In one classroom, a girl is sharpening a pencil.

2. In the gym, students are exercising.

3. In the hall, a boy is opening his locker.

4. In one classroom, two girls are whispering.

5. In the home economics class, students are cooking.

6. In the cafeteria, two boys are fighting.

7. In one classroom, a boy is goofing off.

8. In the hall, a boy is getting a drink.

MEMORY BANK

cooking	getting a drink	sharpening a pencil	exercising
fighting	goofing off	opening his locker	whispering

Using a Pay Telephone

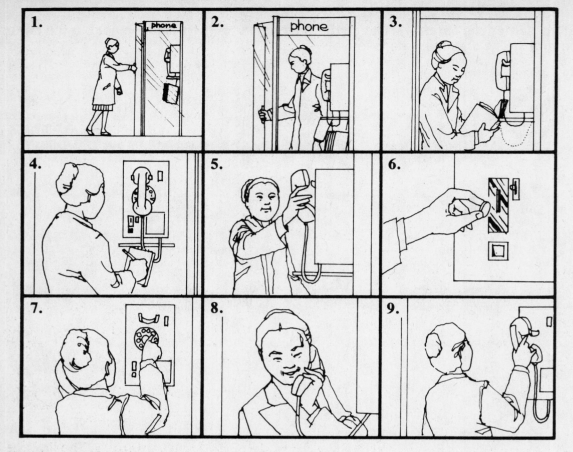

ing." "Number 8." "She is talking (on the phone/to someone)." Repeat this activity for all nine phrases. Provide vocabulary help as needed. Assign the page for independent work.

Write the missing word. The first one is done for you.

1. The woman is _____*entering*_____ the phone booth.

2. She is _____ the door.

3. She is _____ a number in the phone book.

4. She is _____ the number.

5. She is _____ the phone.

6. She is _____ a dime.

7. She is _____ .

8. She is _____ to someone.

9. She is _____ .

Skill Objectives: Using present progressive, sequencing
Teach/review the vocabulary in the Memory Bank. Have a student read one word or phrase. A second student will say the number of the matching picture. A third student will put the word(s) into a complete sentence. Example: "Talk-

─── **MEMORY BANK** ───

talking	dialing	hanging up	picking up	depositing
looking for	writing down	closing	entering	

Skill Sharpeners 1—Unit 8

Circus Time!

Look at the picture. Then answer the questions. Use complete sentences. The first one is done for you.

1. How many clowns are there? _*There are three clowns.*_____

2. How many bears are there? _____

3. How many monkeys are there? _____

4. How many tents are there? _____

5. Are there any elephants? _____

6. How many horses are there? _____

7. How many cowboys and cowgirls are there? _____

8. How many acrobats are there? _____

9. How many children are there? _____

MEMORY BANK
---

acrobats	children	cowboys	elephants	monkeys
bears	clowns	cowgirls	horses	tents

There Is, There Are

A. Fill in the missing word. The first two are done for you.

1. There ____is____ one airport in Boston.

2. There ____are____ ten students in the class.

3. There _____ few cars in the parking lot.

4. There _____ a letter on the table for you.

5. There _____ many universities in Dallas.

6. There _____ a big park in this city.

B. Write the negative sentence. Then write the question. The first one is done for you.

1. There are three banks on Main Street.

   Negative: _There aren't any banks on Main Street._

   Question: _Are there any banks on Main Street?_

2. There are a few letters on the desk.

   Negative: _____

   Question: _____

3. There are two hospitals in Littleton.

   Negative: _____

   Question: _____

4. There are several students from Mexico in my class.

   Negative: _____

   Question: _____

C. Write the question that goes with each answer. The first one is done for you.

1. There are 15 hospitals in Fort Worth.

   Question: _How many hospitals are there in Fort Worth?_

2. There are 14 students from Vietnam in my school.

   Question: _____

3. There are more than seven million people in Los Angeles.

   Question: _____

Skill Objectives: *There is/are,* asking questions, making negative statements

Write on the board: *There is . . . . There are . . . . There aren't any . . . .* Have each student make at least one statement about the school, the class-

room or his/her desk using one of these sentence starters. Then ask a few "How many . . . ?" questions. Let volunteers ask other "How many . . . ?" questions. Go over the entire page as an oral group activity before assigning as independent written work.

Skill Sharpeners 1—Unit 8

Interviewing

A. Interview your teachers, the school secretary, or the assistant principal to find out the answers to these questions.

1. How many students are there in this school? _____

2. How many students are there from Mexico? _____

3. How many classrooms are there? _____

4. How many teachers are there? _____

5. How many librarians are there? _____

6. How many guidance counselors are there? _____

7. How many buses are there? _____

8. Are there any TVs in the school? _____

9. Are there any computers? _____

10. Are there any students from Vietnam? _____

B. Now write a paragraph about your school.

Here are some interesting facts about my school.

_____

_____

_____

_____

_____

_____

_____

_____

_____

Quincy Market

In the city of Boston there are many universities, many students, many people from many different countries, and many good restaurants. In one building in Boston there are four American restaurants, two Italian restaurants, one Greek restaurant, and one Arabic restaurant. This building is called Quincy Market. The building is 150 years old. It is old on the outside, but it is new on the inside.

Quincy Market is part of a big shopping center. All the buildings are old, but there are modern stores in them. There are shoe stores, clothing stores, stores for jewelry, candy, and toys, and many other kinds of stores. Outside, there are places for people to sit and rest and watch the people.

Nearby there is an outdoor market, where you can buy fruit and vegetables. There are fresh red tomatoes, orange carrots, and green cucumbers in the vegetable stands. In the fruit stands there are bananas, apples, oranges, peaches, and plums. There are also butcher shops, cheese shops, and fish shops. You can buy chicken and turkey and duck, beef and lamb and pork, and all kinds of fish and shellfish. Everyone is shouting, trying to get you to buy the things he or she is selling. There is a big difference between an outdoor market and a supermarket!

Quincy Market is a fun place to go! If you like to eat, don't miss it when you go to Boston.

board: *Boston is a city in Massachusetts. Quincy Market is in New York City.* Have the class decide which statement is true and which is false. Ask students to reread the story silently before completing the exercises independently.

Read each sentence below. Write T if the sentence is true. Write F if it is false. The first one is done for you.

1. Boston is a mixture of many different people and cultures. ___T___

2. There are only a few restaurants in the Quincy Market area. _____

3. You can sit outdoors in the Quincy Market area. _____

4. There are new buildings to shop in. _____

5. All the stores in Quincy Market are very old. _____

6. You can buy fresh fruit in the indoor market. _____

7. There are tomatoes and cucumbers in the fruit stands. _____

8. An outdoor market is the same as a supermarket. _____

9. Quincy Market is a very busy place. _____

10. At the outdoor market, you can buy lobsters, shrimps, oysters and clams. _____

11. You can buy meat at a butcher shop. _____

12. It's fun to go to Quincy Market. _____

Skill Objective: Reading for details
Read the selection aloud as students follow along. Explain unfamiliar vocabulary. Have students locate Boston on a U.S. map. Write two sentences on the

Chicago

Mr. Peters is in a taxi. He is coming from O'Hare airport in Chicago. He is going to the North Side of the city. His taxi driver is talking to him.

"Chicago is a great town. I love it. We have two baseball teams here, the Cubs and the White Sox. I like the Cubs. The White Sox are boring and they're losers, too. I never go to their games. But there's a lot more to Chicago than baseball. Look around. We're in the city now. This is Michigan Avenue. There's the John Hancock Center. That building is 100 stories high! That's too high, if you ask me. If there is a fire on the 85th or 90th floor, how are the firemen going to put it out? There's no chance. . . . Look over there. There's a larger build-ing. It's the Sears Tower. That building is 110 stories high! . . . Do you see those round buildings? Those are the Marina City apartments. Those buildings have 60 floors each. Thousands of people live in each one. Imagine that, all those people in two buildings. It's terrible to have so many neighbors. . . . There's the Merchandise Mart. That's another big building. Do you know what's in that building? There are stores, restaurants, a bank, a post office, a radio station and a T.V. station. It's great, but don't ever go there on a Saturday! It's too crowded. . . . Well, here we are. There's plenty more to see in this city. Remember, ask any cab driver about Chicago. We know everything about this town!"

The taxi driver is giving Mr. Peters lots of information. Many things the driver says are FACTS. *Facts are true statements that you can read or check in an encyclopedia or other reference book.* Other things the driver says are OPINIONS. *Opinions are what a person thinks about something.* They are true for the person saying them, but they are not true for everyone. You cannot check them in a reference book. Two people can have completely different OPINIONS about the same FACTS.

Look at each sentence below. If it is a FACT, write FACT next to it. If it is an OPINION, write OPINION next to it.

1. Chicago has two baseball teams. _____

2. The White Sox are a boring team. _____

3. The John Hancock Center is on Michigan Avenue. _____

4. The John Hancock Center is too tall. _____

5. The Sears Tower is 110 stories high. _____

6. Thousands of people live in Marina City Apartments. _____

7. It's terrible to have thousands of neighbors. _____

8. There are many stores and restaurants in the Merchandise Mart. _____

9. The Merchandise Mart is too crowded on Saturday. _____

10. Taxi drivers know all about Chicago. _____

Skill Objective: Distinguishing between fact and opinion
Read the story aloud as students follow along. Have students locate Chicago on a U.S. map. Read the explanation of the difference between a fact and an opinion. Write the following sentences on the board: *Chicago is the largest city in Illinois. Chicago is a great town.* Let students decide which is a fact and which is an opinion, then explain their reasons. Have students reread the story before completing the Fact vs. Opinion exercise. Let students compare and discuss answers.

Dallas

Dallas is a big city in Texas. Dallas is about 1400 miles from New York and about 1300 miles from San Francisco. It is nearly 300 miles from Galveston, but only 28 miles from Fort Worth.

There are many streets in Dallas. There are hundreds of tall buildings, short buildings, old buildings, and new buildings. You can see all of Dallas from one very tall building.

Two small towns are in the middle of Dallas! The towns are University Park and Highland Park. The Trinity River is in the middle of Dallas, too.

There are more than 200 schools and 16 libraries in Dallas. There are 20 radio stations and 6 TV stations. There are more than 100 banks, and hundreds of churches. There are well known stores, big museums, busy theaters, and fine restaurants. And there are nearly a million people in the city, and many more in the suburbs.

Dallas is a very big city! There is lots of traffic and noise. But people like the big stores and restaurants. They like the theaters and the museums. And they love to watch the football games with the Dallas Cowboys!

How about you? How do you like "Big D?"

A. What is the main idea of this story? Circle the right answer.

a. Dallas is far away from New York and San Francisco.

b. There is lots of pollution in Dallas.

c. Dallas is a big, busy city.

d. There are many schools, libraries, and radio and TV stations in Dallas.

B. Write questions to go with the answers.

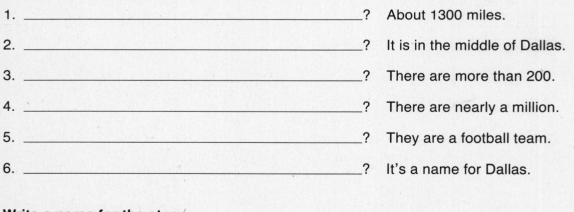

1. _____? About 1300 miles.

2. _____? It is in the middle of Dallas.

3. _____? There are more than 200.

4. _____? There are nearly a million.

5. _____? They are a football team.

6. _____? It's a name for Dallas.

C. Write a name for the story.

_____

D. Now copy the story about Dallas on another piece of paper. Use your best handwriting. Put your name for the story at the top.

Skill Objectives: Identifying main idea and topic, drawing inferences, forming questions
Read the selection aloud. Explain any new words. Have students locate the cities mentioned on a map. Write on the board: *How many . . .? How far . . .?*

What . . .? Where . . .? Have students use these forms to ask questions about the selection. *Part A:* Have students compare their answers and discuss why only one choice states the main idea. If you wish, do Parts B and C as group activities before assigning as written work.

Time Zones

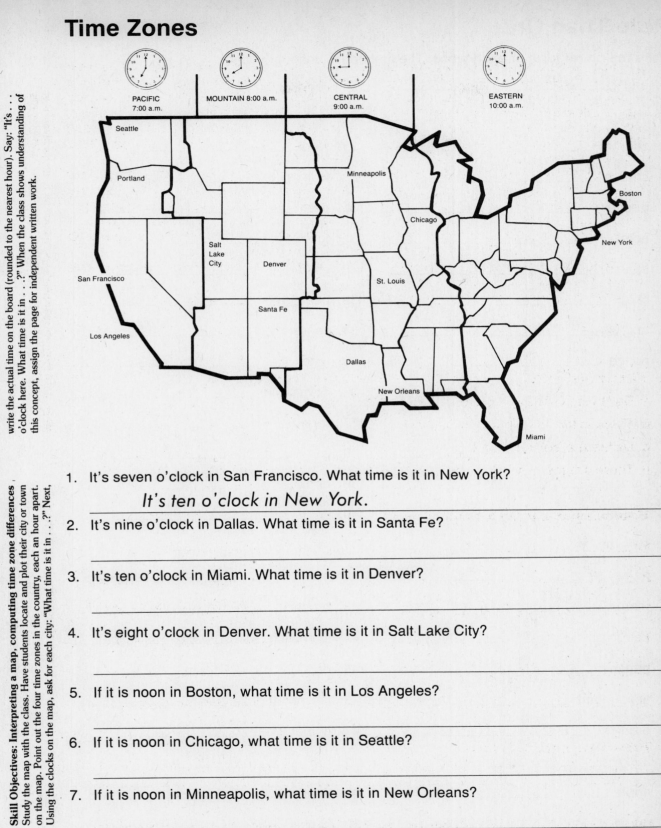

1. It's seven o'clock in San Francisco. What time is it in New York?

   It's ten o'clock in New York.

2. It's nine o'clock in Dallas. What time is it in Santa Fe?

3. It's ten o'clock in Miami. What time is it in Denver?

4. It's eight o'clock in Denver. What time is it in Salt Lake City?

5. If it is noon in Boston, what time is it in Los Angeles?

6. If it is noon in Chicago, what time is it in Seattle?

7. If it is noon in Minneapolis, what time is it in New Orleans?

8. If it is one p.m. in St. Louis, what time is it in Boston?

More Than One

Write the plural form of each word. The first one is done for you.

1. egg _____eggs_____

2. shoe _____

3. country _____

4. church _____

5. bridge _____

6. hotel _____

7. blouse _____

8. chair _____

9. taxi _____

10. peach _____

11. doctor _____

12. suit _____

13. tooth _____

14. shirt _____

15. student _____

16. strawberry _____

17. name _____

18. man _____

19. daughter _____

20. banana _____

21. accountant _____

22. orange _____

23. baby _____

24. apple _____

25. nurse _____

26. jacket _____

27. lawyer _____

28. stool _____

29. woman _____

30. pilot _____

31. foot _____

32. child _____

33. bus _____

34. secretary _____

35. letter _____

36. newspaper _____

37. friend _____

38. belt _____

39. book _____

40. library _____

41. radio _____

42. brother _____

43. brush _____

44. sandwich _____

45. dog _____

46. carrot _____

47. cemetery _____

48. rug _____

49. family _____

50. cousin _____

B. Choose 25 of these words you know well. Write a sentence for each one. Underline the plurals you use in the sentence. For example: "My <u>friends</u> are coming to town."

Skill Objectives: Forming plurals, reviewing vocabulary, writing sentences
All the words on this page appear in Units 1–8 of *New Horizons in English, Book 1.* The page serves as a vocabulary review as well as a review of forming plurals. Do the first ten examples as a group activity, reviewing the rules of plural construction and pronunciation, then assign the page as independent written work. After completing Part B, ask each student to read his/her favorite sentence aloud.

Dear Dot

Dear Dot—

My problem is, my father is never home. He is a sales representative, and he is always going to the airport or the train station or the bus station. He is working in Los Angeles this week. Next week he is going to Chicago. When my father <u>is</u> at home, he is tired, or he is working in his office. What can I do?

Lonely Son

Skill Objectives: Reading comprehension, making judgments
Read the letter aloud as students follow along. Explain any unfamiliar words. Ask students to reread the letter silently, then answer questions 1-5. Correct the first four answers, then let students compare their choice of advice. Read Dot's answer together. Let students tell why they agree or disagree with Dot's solution, and perhaps offer some other suggestions.

1. What's the boy's problem? _____

_____

2. What's his father's occupation? _____

_____

3. What's his father doing this week? _____

4. Where is his father going next week? _____

_____

5. What is your advice for Lonely Son?

   a. Don't bother your father.

   b. Become a salesman too.

   c. Talk with your father about your feelings.

   d. Surprise your father and meet him in Chicago.

6. Now read Dot's answer. See if your answer is the same. If your answer is different, tell why you disagree. Dot's advice is below.

Dear Lonely Son—

Many young people write to me with the same problem. Fathers and mothers are working hard and spending less time with their children. Talk to your father; tell him you want to spend more time with him. Maybe you can go with him on a short trip. Tell him you want to do things with him on the weekends. Remember, he's working hard to take care of you.

Dot

What and Why?

A. Write the letter for the "Why" that goes with each "What." The first one is done for you.

What are they doing?

1. __e__ Maria is buying two pairs of shoes.
2. ____ Angel is taking off his sweater.
3. ____ Dot is putting on her gloves.
4. ____ Francisco is putting on his raincoat.
5. ____ The nurses are putting on their uniforms.
6. ____ Loc is putting on his bathing suit.
7. ____ James and Sandy are wearing wedding rings.
8. ____ Pablo is putting on his boots.

Why are they doing it?

a. They are married.
b. Her hands are very cold.
c. He is going out in the rain.
d. They are going to work.
e. She is at a shoe sale.
f. It's hot in his room.
g. He is going out in the snow.
h. He is going to the beach.

B. What about you? Tell "why." Use complete sentences. The first one is done for you.

1. You are closing the window. *I am closing the window because it's cold.*

2. You are wearing sunglasses. _____

3. You are not going to school. _____

4. You are calling the fire department. _____

5. You are crying. _____

6. You are cleaning your room. _____

7. You are studying. _____

━ MEMORY BANK ━

today is a holiday	my room is messy	it's cold
I have a big test tomorrow	it's very sunny outside	there is a fire down the street
		my best friend is moving away

I am running and *Her hair is wet.* Encourage students to come up with a wide range of possible causes. Do the first few examples in Parts A and B together, then assign the page as independent work.

Skill Objective: Recognizing cause and effect Write and read the sentence: *Yuri is taking off his hat.* Ask: "Why is he taking off his hat?" Let students suggest a variety of reasons: He is in a house/a church. It is very hot, etc. Repeat this cause-effect activity with the sentences:

Crossword Puzzle

Write the words in the right places. Number 1 Across and number 1 Down are done for you.

Across

1. Please _____ down.
4. Guitars make it.
7. Where you get books.
9. Person high up in a circus.
10. Where you sleep.
12. In winter, Gina _____ down the hills.
15. You eat in them.
18. Either this _____ that.
19. What _____ of shop is it?
21. Get _____ of here.
23. New and up to date.
26. Where did she _____?
27. Jim is _____ in the gym.
30. Where you play basketball.
32. The book is _____ the table.
33. Maria is _____ the book.
34. When it is _____, everything is white.

Down

1. Rosa is _____ at my house.
2. Where you probably are now (if you're in school).
3. A new _____ of shoes.
4. That's _____ pencil, not yours.
5. What ice cream and snow are.
6. They were _____ at pictures.
8. What is _____?
11. What happens in 15 across.
13. Have a _____ of coffee.
14. What are you _____ about?
16. You are studying and _____ am I.
17. _____ or false?
20. Will you _____ something for me?
21. Look at that boy _____ there!
22. At that place.
24. What are you _____ tonight?
25. Yes or _____?
28. Brother of a daughter.
29. It makes the car go.
31. Was it a _____ or a woman?

(Answers on page 126)

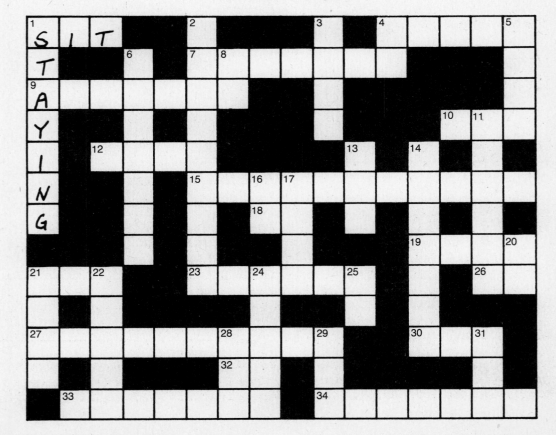

Sentence Structure

STATEMENT	Jim *is* studying English.
YES/NO QUESTION	Is Jim studying English?
SHORT ANSWER	Yes, he *is*.
	No, he *isn't*.

A. Change the sentence to a question. The first one is done for you.

1. Mary is eating an apple.   *Is Mary eating an apple?*

2. We are practicing English.   _____

3. Tom is waiting for the bus.   _____

4. They are living in Boston.   _____

5. I am learning English.   _____

6. The cat is sleeping.   _____

B. Write a short answer. Respond with your own answers.

1. Is your teacher sleeping now?   _____

2. Are you fixing a car now?   _____

3. Is it raining now?   _____

4. Is Maria typing?   _____

5. Are your friends having a party soon?   _____

STATEMENT	Jim is studying English.
YES/NO QUESTION	Is Jim studying English?
WH-QUESTION	*What* is Jim studying?
	Where is Jim studying?
	Why is Jim studying?

C. Answer these questions.

1. Where are you living?   _____

2. What are you doing?   _____

3. Why are you learning English?   _____

Skill Objectives: Asking/answering questions, present progressive
Discuss the sample box. Write some verbs on the board: *working, going, reading, sleeping,* etc. Ask students to use these verbs to make statements about their classmates. ("Jon is sleeping.") Another student should rephrase the sentence as a question and a third provide an answer. *Part C:* Have students answer the wh-questions in the box. After students have independently completed the section, encourage them to share their answers to the three questions.

Where Are You From?

A. Match the countries and nationalities. Write the letter of the nationality name next to the name of the country it goes with. The first one is done for you.

listed to name and locate their countries. Ask their classmates: "What nationality is . . .?" Provide vocabulary as needed. Have students do this page independently, then let each student read one of his/her sentences from Part B aloud to the class.

Country

				Nationality
1.	England	*j*	a.	Peruvian
2.	Ireland		b.	Brazilian
3.	Sweden		c.	Swiss
4.	Japan		d.	Puerto Rican
5.	Canada		e.	Vietnamese
6.	Peru		f.	Turkish
7.	Mexico		g.	Lebanese
8.	Vietnam		h.	Japanese
9.	United States		i.	Russian
10.	Colombia		j.	English
11.	Brazil		k.	Indian
12.	Turkey		l.	American
13.	China		m.	Mexican
14.	Puerto Rico		n.	Chinese
15.	Spain		o.	Swedish
16.	Lebanon		p.	Dutch
17.	Soviet Union		q.	Irish
18.	India		r.	Spanish
19.	Switzerland		s.	Canadian
20.	Holland		t.	Colombian

B. Write sentences about eight of the countries.
Example: (S)he is from England. (S)he is English.

Skill Objective: Naming countries and nationalities
Display a world map. Have students locate each country listed in Part A then ask: "What do we call people from (Colombia)?" "Is anyone in this class from Colombia?" ("Yes, Elena is Colombian.") Ask students whose countries are not

1. _____

2. _____

3. _____

4. _____

5. _____

6. _____

7. _____

8. _____

My Country and Yours

Ireland is a small country in the North Atlantic. It is near England. Ireland is famous for many things. It is famous for its green countryside. In some parts of Ireland there are miles and miles of rolling, green fields. Other parts of Ireland are gray and rocky. Sometimes the weather in Ireland is chilly and damp. It rains a lot in Ireland; that's one reason the fields are so green.

Dublin is the capital of Ireland. Dublin is a beautiful old city. There are many small squares and parks in Dublin. O'Connell Street, in the center of Dublin, is very wide. There are fine stores on it. There is a very famous university in the city. It is called Trinity College.

The Irish people love to sing and dance and tell stories. I'm Irish; Ireland is my home. I think it's a wonderful country.

A. Answer each of the questions below. Use short answers. The first one is done for you.

1. Where is Ireland? _*It's in the North Atlantic.*_____

2. What country is Ireland near? _____

3. What is the capital of Ireland? _____

4. What university is in Dublin? _____

5. What do the Irish love to do? _____

_____

B. Now write about your country. Use more paper if you need to.

_____
_____
_____
_____
_____
_____
_____
_____
_____

Skill Objectives: Reading for details, writing an informative essay
Read the selection aloud as students follow along. Explain unfamiliar words. Have students reread the text silently. Discuss some or all of the comprehension questions, then assign the page as independent work. Students should use the text as a model as they write original essays about their native countries. Allow time for students to read their paragraphs aloud to the class.

Pronouns

A. Finish these conversations. Fill in the missing words.

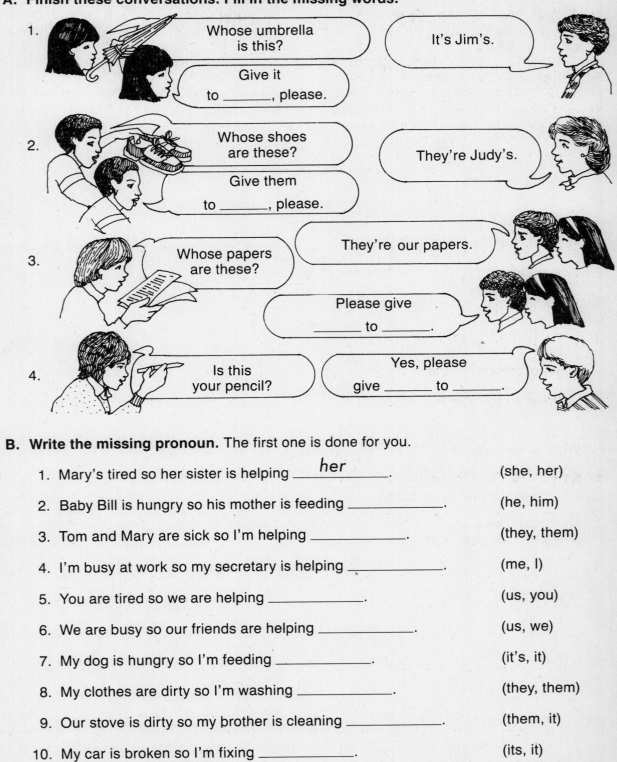

1. Whose umbrella is this?

   Give it to _____, please.

   It's Jim's.

2. Whose shoes are these?

   Give them to _____, please.

   They're Judy's.

3. Whose papers are these?

   They're our papers.

   Please give _____ to _____.

4. Is this your pencil?

   Yes, please give _____ to _____.

B. Write the missing pronoun. The first one is done for you.

1. Mary's tired so her sister is helping _*her*_____.   (she, her)

2. Baby Bill is hungry so his mother is feeding _____.   (he, him)

3. Tom and Mary are sick so I'm helping _____.   (they, them)

4. I'm busy at work so my secretary is helping _____.   (me, I)

5. You are tired so we are helping _____.   (us, you)

6. We are busy so our friends are helping _____.   (us, we)

7. My dog is hungry so I'm feeding _____.   (it's, it)

8. My clothes are dirty so I'm washing _____.   (they, them)

9. Our stove is dirty so my brother is cleaning _____.   (them, it)

10. My car is broken so I'm fixing _____.   (its, it)

Skill Objectives: Using pronouns and possessives
Write these sentences on the board: *Give the book to Ann. Give the money to Jim and Ed. Give the cards to Maria and me.* Underline the direct object. Have a student repeat each sentence using the pronoun replacement. ("Give it to Ann.") Underline the indirect object. Have a student substitute both pronouns. Then ask: "Whose book is it?" ("It's Ann's.") Have students read and complete Part A orally. Do some or all of Part B aloud before assigning as written work.

Dear Dot

Dear Dot—

I am Vietnamese. There are no other Vietnamese kids in my school. I don't fit in here. I still don't speak English very well, and I feel stupid when I make mistakes. There are some girls I want to know, but I am too shy to talk to them. I am not happy, and I miss my country. What can I do?

Homesick and Sad

1. Where is the student from? _____

2. How many Vietnamese students are there in her school? _____

3. What language is she learning? _____

4. When does she feel stupid? _____

_____

5. Who does she want to know? _____

_____

6. What is your advice for Homesick and Sad? Circle your answer.

   a. Learn more English and make more friends.   c. Get a job.

   b. Go back to your own country.   d. Read more and watch television.

7. Now read Dot's answer. See if your answer is the same. If your answer is different, tell why you disagree. Dot's advice is below.

Dear Homesick and Sad—

Join a club or another kind of extra-curricular activity. Invite the girls you want to know to your house. Don't be so shy—ask them to help you practice your English. Teach them some words in Vietnamese. Then they will understand how hard English can be for you. Don't be afraid to ask for more help from other students and your teachers. Most people are happy to help if they know what your problem is.

Dot

Skill Objectives: Reading comprehension, making judgments
Read the letter aloud as students follow along. Explain any unfamiliar words.
Ask students to reread the letter silently, then answer questions 1–6. Correct
the first five answers, then let students compare their choice of advice. Read
Dot's answer together. Let students tell why they agree or disagree with Dot's
solution and perhaps offer some different suggestions of their own.

Watch the Clock

What time is it? Write the sentence. The first one is done for you.

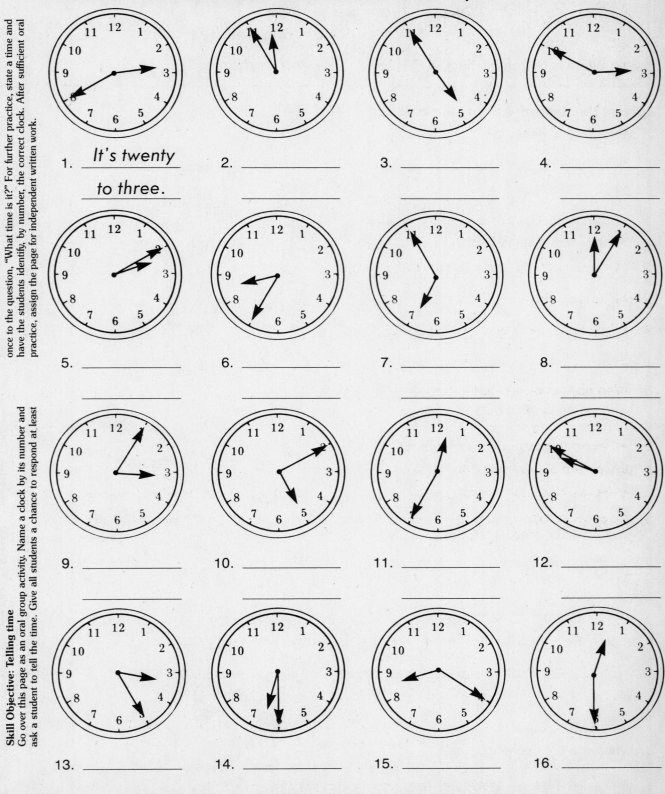

1. _It's twenty to three._

2. _____

3. _____

4. _____

5. _____

6. _____

7. _____

8. _____

9. _____

10. _____

11. _____

12. _____

13. _____

14. _____

15. _____

16. _____

Where Are They Going?

Where's Peter going?		He's going to the bus station.
Why?		He's going to meet a friend.
When is he coming back?		He's coming back at 9:00.

Look at the picture. Answer the questions.

1. Where's she going?

   _____

   Why?

   _____

   When is she coming back?

   _____

2. Where's he going?

   _____

   Why?

   _____

   When is he coming back?

   _____

3. Where are you going?

   _____

   Why?

   _____

   When are you coming back?

   _____

4. Where are they going?

   _____

   Why?

   _____

   When are they coming back?

   _____

Skill Objectives: Using present progressive, using *going to*, as future form, drawing inferences

Study the example box with the class. Be sure students understand how to use the information in the picture cues. Cover the page as an oral group activity.

Answers to "Why?" should vary and provide a springboard for discussion about the different reasons people go to various places. Assign the page for written work.

Going Places and Doing Things

Read each paragraph carefully. Where are the people going? Write the name of the place.

Skill Objectives: Understanding uses of *going*, *going to*, drawing conclusions

Teach/review the vocabulary in the Memory Bank. For each place, ask: "What do people do at/in a(n) . . .?" Do the first one or two examples as a group exercise, then assign as independent written work.

1. Many people are going here this morning. They are going to deposit money, cash checks, and pay bills. Where are these people going?

   _____

2. Other people are going here. They are going to sit in the sun, swim, and dive. Where are they going?

   _____

3. At this place people are going to go to class, to the library, to meet their friends, and to study. Where are they going?

   _____

4. At this place, people are going to read, take out and return books, and do homework. Where are they going?

   _____

5. Some people are going here to pick up packages. Others are going to mail letters and to buy stamps. Where are all these people going?

   _____

6. At this place people are going to buy drinks and candy, eat popcorn, and sit in the dark. Where are they going?

   _____

7. Many people are going here today. Some are going to buy meat and cheese. Others are buying milk and vegetables. Where are these people going?

   _____

8. At this place, people are going to buy flowers, visit sick friends, get X-rays and prescriptions. Where are they going?

   _____

9. Some people are going here to meet friends. Other people are going on vacations. They are all going to see many large planes. Where are these people going?

   _____

10. People are going here in their cars. They are going to buy gasoline and fill their tires with air. Some of them will talk to mechanics about their cars. Where are these people going?

   _____

━━ MEMORY BANK ━━

airport	**beach**	**grocery store**	**library**	**post office**
bank	**gas station**	**hospital**	**movie theater**	**school**

A Trip to the "Big Apple"

Tom is going to the airport at 10:00. He's taking his suitcase and his ticket. Tom is taking a vacation in New York City. His mother is going with him. They are going to stay in a nice hotel in Manhattan.

The first thing they are going to do in New York is visit the World Trade Center. The World Trade Center is the tallest building in New York City. Tom and his mother are going to eat lunch in the restaurant on the top floor.

What else are they going to do? They're going to take the bus to the Metropolitan Museum and then the subway to the Empire State Building. They're going to ride the ferry to the Statue of Liberty. Tom is going to climb all 168 steps to the top! Tom and his mother are going to have a good time in "the Big Apple."

A. What is this story mostly about? Circle the answer.

a. Tom's mother

b. Airplanes and airports

c. A vacation in New York City

d. Climbing the Statue of Liberty

B. Answer these questions.

1. How are Tom and his mother traveling to New York? _____

_____

2. Where are they going to sleep while they're in New York? _____

_____

3. What is "the Big Apple?" _____

_____

C. Write the questions. Then practice asking and answering with a classmate.

1. _____ He's going to the airport.

2. _____ His mother is.

3. _____ The World Trade Center is.

4. _____ They're going to ride the ferry.

5. _____ There are 168.

Skill Objectives: Identifying main idea, making inferences, asking questions
Read the text aloud as students follow along. Explain any new vocabulary. Have students reread the selection silently before answering the questions.

Depending on the skill level of your group, you may wish to discuss the questions as a group before assigning as independent work. If students work independently, be sure to discuss and compare answers after completion.

A Field Trip

Mr. Beck is a history teacher in Rapid City, South Dakota. South Dakota is a state in the Midwest. Tomorrow, he and his class are going on a field trip. They are going to the Black Hills, the mountains of South Dakota. They are going to see the faces of four American Presidents: George Washington, Thomas Jefferson, Abraham Lincoln, and Theodore Roosevelt. They are not going to see the Presidents themselves, but they are not going to see pictures or photographs of the Presidents either. They are going to see the Presidents' faces in the mountains!

An artist named Gutzon Borglum carved the stone faces. They are 60 feet high and are a part of Mount Rushmore, a mountain in the Black Hills. The faces are so big that you can see them 60 miles away. Mr. Beck's students are going to take pictures and write stories about their visit. If you ever travel across the country, make sure you visit this famous monument.

A. Answer the following questions. Use short answers. The first one is done for you.

1. Where is South Dakota? _____*in the Midwest*_____

2. What is Mr. Beck's class going to do tomorrow? _____

3. Where is the class going? _____

4. What are they going to see? _____

5. What did Gutzon Borglum do? _____

6. How big are the faces? _____

7. What are Mr. Beck's students going to do on the trip? _____

_____

8. At what distance can you see the faces of the Presidents? _____

B. What is this story mostly about? Circle the best answer.

a. the Presidents

b. Mr. Beck's class

c. Mount Rushmore

d. North Dakota

Dear Dot

Dear Dot—

My problem is this. I like a girl in my class, but she doesn't know I exist. She is very popular. She is always going to a party or the movies or the arcade with her girlfriends. I'm going to ask her out, but I'm very nervous. I don't know what to say or how to act. And what if she says no? I'm afraid of looking stupid.

Silent Admirer

1. Is the girl in the boy's class? _____

2. Is she popular? _____

3. What is he going to do? _____

4. What is he afraid of? _____

5. What is your advice for Silent Admirer? Circle your answer.

   a. Send her a letter.

   b. Ask one of her friends if she likes you.

   c. Be confident; don't worry about her answer.

   d. Forget about her; ask a different girl.

6. Now read Dot's answer. See if your answer is the same. If your answer is different, tell why you disagree. Dot's advice is below.

Dear Silent Admirer—

Don't be afraid of looking stupid. Have more confidence in yourself. So what if she says no the first time you ask her out? You can ask her again. And remember, many girls are probably going to say no to you in the future! So get used to it!

Dot

Skill Objectives: Reading comprehension, making judgments Read the letter aloud as students follow along. Explain any unfamiliar words. Ask students to reread the letter silently, then answer questions 1–5. Correct the first four answers, then let students compare their choice of advice. Read Dot's answer together. Let students tell why they agree or disagree with Dot's solution, and perhaps offer some other suggestions.

What Do You Have to Do?

A. Bill has some problems. Write what he *has to* do to solve his problems. The first one is done for you.

1. Bill's room is messy. _He has to clean his room._

2. The dishes are dirty. _____

3. His clothes are on the bed. _____

4. The car is dirty. _____

5. The waste baskets are full. _____

6. It's time for dinner. _____

7. The rugs are dirty. _____

8. The dog is hungry. _____

MEMORY BANK

feed the dog	wash the car	wash the dishes	hang up his clothes
set the table	empty the waste baskets	vacuum the rugs	clean his room

B. Here are some more problems. Write what the people *have to* do to solve the problems. The first one is done for you.

Problems	Solutions
1. They have an English test tomorrow.	_They have to study._

2. My bike is broken. _____

3. Susan is very sick. _____

4. My father's birthday is tomorrow. _____

5. There is no milk in my refrigerator. _____

6. John is coming to a red light. _____

7. They are going to Paris soon. _____

8. Our car is out of gas. _____

MEMORY BANK

call the doctor	buy some milk	buy a present	stop the car
get passports	go to a gas station	study	fix my bike

Skill Objectives: Using have to, has to, *drawing conclusions*
Part A: Teach/review the phrases in the Memory Bank. Have a volunteer mime one of the actions. Ask the class: "What does (Luis) have to do?" ("He has to set the table.") Repeat for all eight expressions. Read the directions. Do one or two examples with the class, then have students work independently. *Part B:* Teach/review vocabulary in the Memory Bank. Do the exercise orally before assigning as independent work. Listen for use of the correct pronoun and verb form.

Can and Can't

A. Read the question and look at the picture. Then answer the question. The first one is done for you.

1. What sport can he play?

He can play soccer.

2. What instrument can she play?

3. What game can they play?

4. What sport can you play?

5. What instrument can they play?

B. Now write a story about yourself. What can you do? What can't you do? Use more paper if you need to.

Skill Objectives: Using modals: *can/can't*, writing a paragraph *Part A:* Do this section as an oral group activity before assigning as written work. *Part B:* Write the following questions on the board: *What sports can you play? What games can you play? What instruments can you play? What languages can you speak? Can you ride a bike? Can you type? Can you make coffee?* Have students suggest other *Can you . . .?* questions, then discuss what they can and can't do. Encourage students to read their finished paragraphs aloud.

Interviewing

Interview two classmates. Write their names above the two columns. Then write their answers in the box. Report your findings to the class.

Name: THINGS PEOPLE DO	STUDENT 1	STUDENT 2
1. Can you skate?		
2. Can you play the guitar?		
3. Can you dance?		
4. Can you play Ping-Pong?		
5. Can you run a mile?		
6. Can you speak Spanish?		
7. Can you play chess?		
8. Can you swim?		
9. Can you cook?		
10. Can you play the drums?		
11. Can you ski?		
12. Can you play soccer?		
13. Can you type?		
14. Can you drive?		
15. Can you ride a horse?		
16. Can you fix a car?		

Skill Objectives: Using modals: *can/can't,* **using a chart**
Teach/review the vocabulary on this page, then divide the class into groups of four. Each student should interview two other students from his/her group.

Odd Man Out

A. Odd Man Out. Circle the word that doesn't belong.

1. ironing, washing, skating, cleaning
2. dishes, laundry, trash, tennis
3. soccer, piano, drums, flute
4. bathroom, kitchen, bedroom, laundromat
5. mall, airport, bank, bedroom
6. gloves, bathing suit, sun, pool
7. nervous, lonely, homesick, flute
8. typewriter, paper, chair, eraser

B. Draw a line to the matching set of words.

1. Tennis	a. bat, strike, glove, foul
2. Soccer	b. hearts, diamond, clubs, spades
3. Baseball	c. keys, strings, pedals
4. Checkers	d. strings, pick
5. Cards	e. net, racket, ball, court
6. Chess	f. dice, jail, go, Boardwalk
7. Piano	g. King, Pawn, Knight, Queen
8. Guitar	h. goal, kick, field, goalie
9. Monopoly	i. black, red, jump
10. Skiing	j. poles, snow, downhill, cross country

Skill Objective: Classifying
Part A: Have students explain why *skating* does not belong in the first set of words. Let students work independently or in pairs with the remaining items, then compare and discuss answers as a group. *Part B:* Do this as a group activity or assign for independent work and discuss afterwards. Remind students that if they cannot solve one item, they should skip it and do the items they can. Then they can return to the difficult items and see which answer choices remain.

A Bike Trip

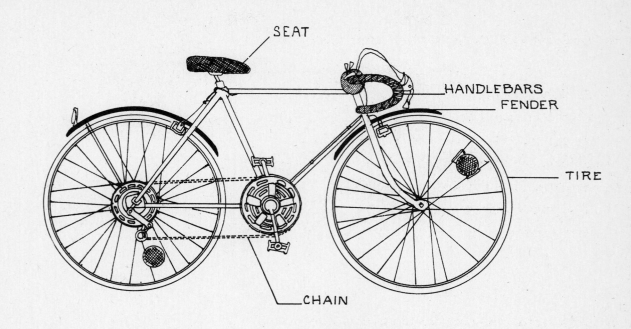

SEAT

HANDLEBARS
FENDER

TIRE

CHAIN

It's early in the morning and Peter is at the gas station. He's getting his bicycle ready for a long trip. He's polishing the handlebars. He's putting fresh grease on the chain. He's filling the tires with air. He's tightening the seat. Now he's ready to go.

This is Peter's first trip of the summer. He's a good rider. He's going to Crystal Lake. Crystal Lake is thirty miles away from Peter's house. Peter and his friends are riding to the lake together. They are going to stay there all day. At 6:00 they are going to ride home.

Answer these questions. The first one is done for you.

1. Where is Peter early in the morning? *He is at the gas station.*

2. What is he doing to the handlebars of his bike? _____

3. What is he doing to the chain? _____

4. What is he doing to the tires? _____

5. What is he doing to the seat? _____

6. Where is Peter going? _____

7. Where is Crystal Lake? _____

8. Who is going with Peter? _____

9. When is Peter coming home? _____

Jack's Car

Jack is going to drive to the rock concert. This is his car.

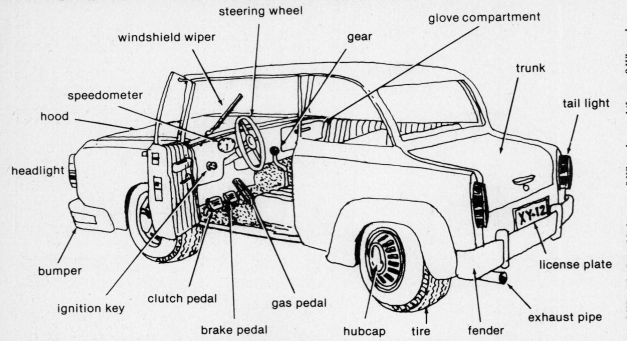

Skill Objectives: Interpreting a diagram, drawing inferences, writing a paragraph
Study the car diagram with the class. Ask questions about the labeled parts: "When do you use the windshield wipers/the headlights? How do you start/ stop a car? When do the tail lights go on? When do you shift gears? Where do you keep maps/your spare tire?" Part A: Teach any new vocabulary, then assign for independent work. Part B: If possible, display magazine pictures of cars. If they wish, students may choose one of these pictures to describe.

A. In the column at the right are some parts of Jack's car. Decide what each part does. Read the sentences on the left. Draw a line from the sentence to the part of the car that Jack will use. The first one is done for you.

1. It is raining.
2. It is getting dark.
3. It says 50 MPH.
4. Jack is stopping at a light.
5. Jack is shifting.
6. Jack is starting his car.
7. Jack is accelerating.

a. speedometer
b. brake pedal
c. windshield wipers
d. headlights
e. gas pedal
f. ignition key
g. gear

B. Now write about your car. If you don't have a car, write about your dream car. Tell as much as you can about it. What kind is it? What color is it? Is it old or new? How big is it? Use more paper if you need to.

_____

_____

_____

_____

_____

_____

Lorena's Car

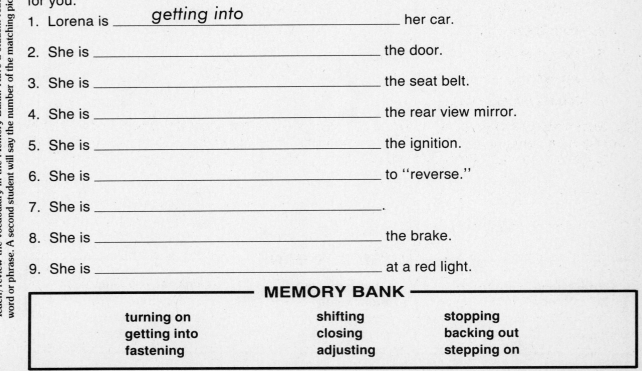

Lorena is driving to work. Look at the pictures. Then read the sentences that tell about them. Complete each sentence with words from the Memory Bank. The first one is done for you.

1. Lorena is _____ *getting into* _____ her car.

2. She is _____ the door.

3. She is _____ the seat belt.

4. She is _____ the rear view mirror.

5. She is _____ the ignition.

6. She is _____ to "reverse."

7. She is _____.

8. She is _____ the brake.

9. She is _____ at a red light.

━━ MEMORY BANK ━━

turning on	**shifting**	**stopping**
getting into	**closing**	**backing out**
fastening	**adjusting**	**stepping on**

Road Signs

Use words from the Memory Bank to tell what the signs mean. The first one is done for you.

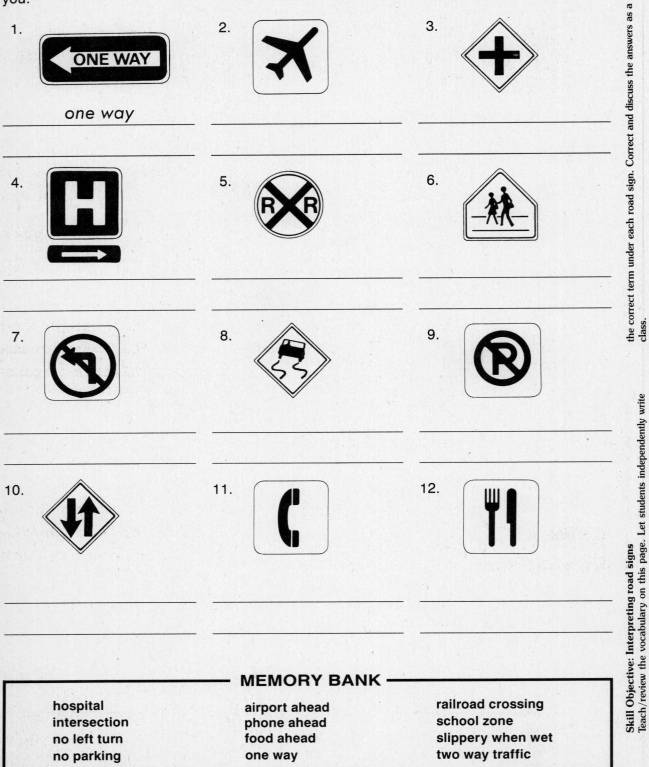

1.

one way

2.

3.

4.

5.

6.

7.

8.

9.

10.

11.

12.

Skill Objective: Interpreting road signs
Teach/review the vocabulary on this page. Let students independently write the correct term under each road sign. Correct and discuss the answers as a class.

More Road Signs

Circle the traffic rule that goes with each sign. The first one is done for you.

a. You have to stop. (circled)
b. You can stop.
c. You can't stop.

a. You can't turn left.
b. You have to turn left.
c. You can turn left.

a. You can't turn right.
b. You have to turn right.
c. You can turn right.

a. You have to slip in the rain.
b. Careful! You can slip in the rain.
c. This road is always wet.

a. You can drive more than 55 mph.
b. You have to drive more than 55 mph.
c. You can't drive more than 55 mph.

a. You can get gas ahead.
b. You can't get gas ahead.
c. You have to get gas ahead.

a. You can drive both ways on this street.
b. You can only drive one way on this street.
c. You have to drive both ways on this street.

a. You can pass other cars.
b. You have to pass other cars.
c. You have to stay behind other cars.

a. You have to watch for children.
b. You have to cross the street.
c. You can drive quickly.

a. You can park here.
b. You can't park here.
c. You have to park here.

Dear Dot

Dear Dot—

    This is my problem. Ernesto, my brother, is good at everything. He can sing and dance and play the drums, and can speak <u>three</u> languages. Our friends call him "Ernesto the Great" or "Ernesto the Champ." I can write good stories, and I can play the guitar. How can I get people to pay attention to the things I am good at?

Little Brother Juan

1. What is Juan's problem? _____

_____

2. Name three things Ernesto can do. _____

_____

3. What can Juan do? _____

_____

4. What is your advice for Juan? Circle your answer.

   a. Fight with Ernesto.

   b. Change your last name.

   c. Try and do all the things Ernesto does.

   d. Show people the things you can do well.

5. Now read Dot's answer. See if your answer is the same. If your answer is different, tell why you disagree. Dot's advice is below.

Dear Juan—

    Sometimes it's hard to be a little brother (and a little sister). Send your stories to the school newspaper. Take your guitar to parties. Ask Ernesto to teach you to dance. Be patient. Have confidence in what <u>you</u> can do.

Dot

Skill Objectives: Reading comprehension, making judgments
Read the letter aloud as students follow along. Explain any unfamiliar words.
Ask students to reread the letter silently, then answer questions 1–4. Correct the first three answers, then let students compare their choice of advice. Read Dot's answer together. Let students tell why they agree or disagree with Dot's solution, and perhaps offer some other suggestions.

Parts of the Body

A. Write the name of each body part on the line.

10. *head*

11. _____

12. _____

13. _____

14. _____

15. _____

9. _____

8. _____

7. _____

6. _____

5. _____

4. _____

3. _____

2. _____

1. _____

16. _____

17. _____

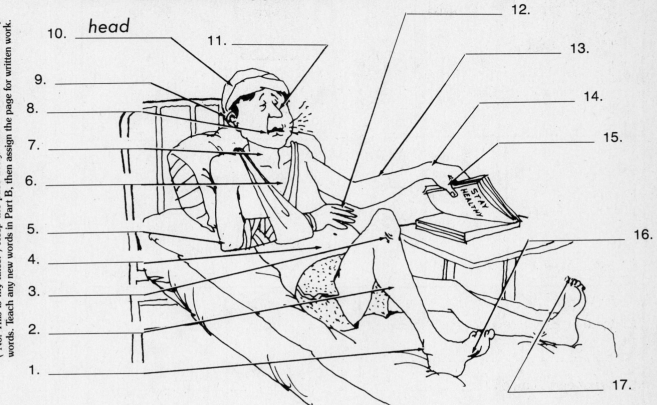

MEMORY BANK

ankle	finger	leg	throat
arm	foot	mouth	thumb
chest	head	nose	toe
ear	knee	stomach	wrist
elbow			

B. If you don't feel well, you must take care of yourself. Draw a line to the matching sentence.

1. She has a headache.

2. She has a toothache.

3. He has a broken arm.

4. The dogs are sick.

5. Mr. Smith is very sick.

The doctor is taking an X-ray.

She is going to the dentist.

She is taking some aspirin.

He is staying in the hospital for two more weeks.

Mother is taking them to the vet.

A Visit to the Doctor

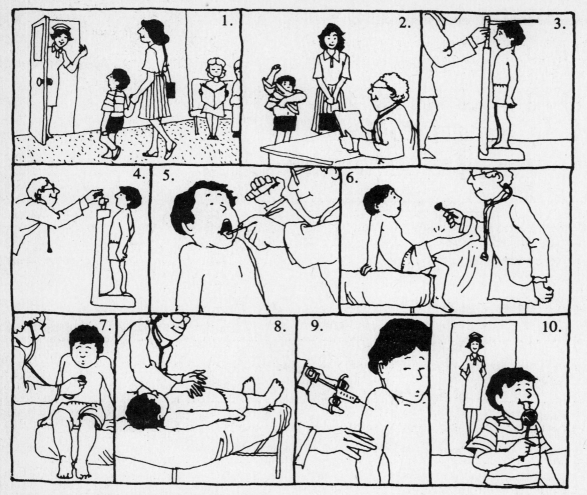

The words on the board will be useful. You may want to introduce the phrase, "test his reflexes." After sufficient discussion, assign the page for independent work. Later, have students read the sentences aloud and discuss their answers.

Skill Objectives: Building vocabulary, sequencing Write on the board: *checking, measuring, height, weight.* Explain the words if necessary. Have students cover the text and look at the pictures only. Introduce the boy as "Bobby." Ask students to discuss what is happening in each picture.

Match the sentences to the pictures.

_____5_____ The doctor is looking down Bobby's throat.

_____ Bobby is taking off his clothes.

_____ The doctor is measuring Bobby's height.

_____ The doctor is giving Bobby a shot.

_____ Bobby is going into the doctor's office.

_____ The doctor is hitting Bobby's knee to test his reflexes.

_____ Bobby is leaving the doctor's office.

_____ The doctor is checking Bobby's weight.

_____ Bobby is lying down so the doctor can check his stomach.

_____ The doctor is listening to Bobby's heart.

How's the Weather?

People are always talking about the weather. Read these quotations and tell what the weather is like. The first one is done for you.

1. "We can go skiing tomorrow."

   It's snowing. _____

2. "The sky is gray and dark. You can't see the sun."

   _____

3. "I'm not taking my umbrella, but I am wearing my raincoat."

   _____

4. "Look, a hat is flying down the street."

   _____

5. "I'm not wearing my coat today. My jacket is fine for this weather."

   _____

6. "Listen to me, Billy. You have to wear your gloves and hat and coat today."

   _____

7. "Look at the thermometer. It's 105°F. Wow!"

   _____

8. "Oh my goodness, you are wet all over. Your shoes and socks are wet too!"

   _____

9. "The bright light hurts my eyes. I have to wear my dark glasses."

   _____

10. "We can't play baseball today. The field is wet and muddy."

    _____

MEMORY BANK

cloudy	drizzling	pouring	snowing	warm
cold	hot	raining	sunny	windy

Skill Objectives: Building vocabulary, making inferences
Teach/review the weather vocabulary in the Memory Bank. Do the first one or two examples orally as a group, then assign the page for independent work. Have students discuss their answers.

Ellen's Calendar

	SUN.	MON.	TUES.	WED.	THURS.	FRI.	SAT.
NOVEMBER							1
	2	3 DENTIST 10:30	4	5	6	7 HAIR- DRESSER 3:00	8
	9	10	VETERANS' DAY 11 HOLIDAY!	12	13	14	15 PARTY!!! 9:00
	16	17	18	19 DOCTOR 9:00	20	21	22
	23 / 30	24	25	26	27 THANKSGIVING DAY	28 NO SCHOOL!	29

events marked on the calendar. "When is Ellen going to the doctor? What time is her appointment?" After sufficient oral practice, assign the page for independent written work.

Skill Objectives: Reading a calendar, reviewing ordinal numbers
Review the days of the week and ordinal numbers. Teach any new vocabulary on the calendar. Encourage students to ask each other questions about the

A. Fill in the missing information.

1. The holiday on November eleventh is _____ .

2. The holiday on November twenty-seventh is _____ .

3. The first Monday in November is the _____ .

4. November twelfth is a _____ .

B. Write the answers.

1. What day is Ellen's dentist appointment? _It's on Monday the third._

2. What time is Ellen's dentist appointment? _____

3. What day is her doctor appointment? _____

4. What time is her doctor apointment? _____

C. Write the questions.

1. _____ ?   On November 15th.

2. _____ ?   At 9:00 p.m.

The Dinner Party

It is 7:55. The Smiths are coming to dinner at 8:00. Gina and Frank are not ready for the Smiths. They want everything to be perfect when the Smiths arrive. Mr. Smith is Frank's boss.

"Hurry, Frank, the Smiths are coming soon. We have to set the table. Bring in the dishes, please. I already have the bowls for the salad and the cups for the coffee. I don't have the knives, forks, and spoons. Bring those with the dishes.

I have to put the tablecloth on the table and find the good napkins. Hurry, Frank, there's so much to do!"

"I'm coming," says Frank. Frank is carrying the dishes, the knives, the forks, and the spoons. He and Gina begin to set the table. Everything is ready. It is 8:00. At 8:01, the Smiths knock on the door. Gina and Frank answer the door together. They are ready for their perfect evening.

A. Answer the following questions. Use short answers. The first one is done for you.

1. When are the Smiths coming to dinner? _____ *8:00* _____

2. Who is Mr. Smith? _____

3. Are Gina and Frank ready for the Smiths at 7:55? _____

4. What do Gina and Frank have to do? _____

5. What does Frank have to bring? _____

6. What does Gina have already? _____

7. What does Gina have to put on the table? _____

8. What does she have to find? _____

9. What time is it when everything is ready? _____

10. When do the Smiths knock on the door? _____

B. What is the main idea of this story? Circle the best answer.

a. Frank's boss is coming.

b. Gina and Frank are having a perfect evening.

c. Frank and Gina are getting ready for a party.

d. Gina has to find the napkins.

C. Talk about these questions.

1. Why do Gina and Frank want everything to be perfect when the Smiths arrive?

2. Is Frank a good husband? Why or why not?

3. Do the Smiths come too early? Explain your answer.

Skill Objectives: Identifying main idea and detail, drawing inferences, making judgments
Read the story aloud as students follow along. Explain any new vocabulary. Have students reread the text silently, then answer the questions in Parts A and B. Correct Part A together and let students discuss why "getting ready for a party" is the only correct answer to Part B. Use the questions in Part C as springboards for class discussion.

Dear Dot

Dear Dot—

The Smiths are coming for dinner this Sunday. I like the Smiths, but they always talk about their health problems. They talk about their headaches and their backaches or stomach problems or sore throats. I don't like that kind of conversation, especially at the dinner table. I like to talk about movies, books, and the news. What can I do?

Healthy

1. Who is coming to dinner? _____

2. When are they coming to dinner? _____

3. What kind of health problems do they talk about? _____

_____

4. What does Healthy like to talk about? _____

_____

5. What is your advice for Healthy?

   a. Tell the Smiths not to come.

   b. Talk about your own problems.

   c. Tell the Smiths to be quiet and not to talk about their problems.

   d. Listen to their problems for a few minutes and then change the subject.

6. Now read Dot's answer. See if your answer is the same. If your answer is different, tell why you disagree. Dot's advice is below.

Dear Healthy—

Many people like to talk about their aches and pains. You have to listen for a little while but not for too long. Make sure you have lots of other ideas to talk about. If the Smiths talk too much about their problems, be ready to change the subject FAST.

Good luck,
Dot

Skill Objectives: Reading comprehension, making judgments
Read the letter aloud as students follow along. Explain any unfamiliar words.
Ask students to reread the letter silently, then answer questions 1-4. Correct the first three answers, then let students compare their choice of advice. Read Dot's answer together. Let students tell why they agree or disagree with Dot's solution and perhaps offer some other suggestions.

Vocabulary Review

Complete each sentence with a word from the Memory Bank.

duced in *New Horizons in English, Book 1.* Familiar formats are used so that students can work independently on these pages.

1. Don't sit on the chair; sit on the _____.

2. I'm sorry but I forget your _____.

3. Bob is wearing a _____ because it's cool today.

4. Maria is _____ breakfast with her friends today.

5. I can't read this; where are my _____?

6. Your shoes are _____ the bed.

7. The boys are watching television in the _____.

8. Don't be nervous; the test is _____.

9. He can play checkers, but he can't play _____.

10. The girls are on a diet; they want to be _____.

11. I can't read any more; my _____ hurt me.

12. He is having a ham and cheese _____ for lunch.

13. Your friends are _____ all the lemonade.

14. The teachers are in the office; they are speaking with the _____.

15. Sally is paying the _____ now.

16. The president of the class is a _____ person.

17. Her _____ color is green.

18. I'm going to bed; I'm _____.

19. The baby is cold; please _____ the window.

20. Luis is _____ his brother a new coat for his birthday.

Vocabulary Review
The following eight pages present a cumulative review of the vocabulary intro-

---

MEMORY BANK

friendly	cards	easy	drinking	thin	tired	eating
close	sweater	eyes	under	buying	glasses	sofa
principal	name	favorite	sandwich	bedroom	cashier	

Vocabulary Review

Complete each sentence with a word from the Memory Bank.

1. The teacher is playing the _____, and the students are singing.

2. The plane is landing at the _____ at ten-thirty.

3. They park their car in the _____ at night.

4. The baby is _____; we have to be quiet.

5. Everyone is _____ to Paul's new record album.

6. The girls are going to the _____; they are going to withdraw some money.

7. We are staying at a large _____ in Dallas.

8. The musicians at that _____ are fantastic.

9. You have to go to the dentist on Friday _____ .

10. I am going to the party _____ my cousins.

11. There are a _____ years in a century.

12. I have to _____ my shoes; they're dirty.

13. The secretaries are _____ the letters now.

14. Are you _____ for the bus too?

15. Joanne can't go to the movies; she has to _____ her room.

16. Your _____ is a mess; you have to comb it.

17. She's wearing two pairs of socks because her _____ are always cold.

18. It's a _____ day; not very sunny at all.

19. The children like to eat a _____ after school.

20. We are having a great vacation; the _____ is wonderful.

Vocabulary Review. See annotation on page 115.

MEMORY BANK

clean	bank	afternoon	typing	listening	guitar	hundred
weather	waiting		with	airport	cloudy	garage
hotel	snack	polish	toes	sleeping	hair	concert

Skill Sharpeners 1—Vocabulary Review

Vocabulary Review

Complete each sentence with a word from the Memory Bank.

1. Men and _____ play on that baseball team.

2. The students are writing the sentences in their _____.

3. _____ is Fred's birthday.

4. His father is the manager of the _____ on Huron Street.

5. People all over the world play _____.

6. I'm going to the _____; I have to buy stamps.

7. Don't write with a _____; use a pencil.

8. Everyone is going to Fred's birthday _____ tonight.

9. It's three _____; we have to go.

10. Pamela is sick; take her to the _____.

11. Do you like _____ in your coffee?

12. There are _____ books in the school library.

13. It's very _____ today. It's 98°F.

14. I don't understand these problems; can you _____ me?

15. This _____ is too small for your head.

16. His aunt and _____ are going to Chicago.

17. Maria and Pedro like baseball; it's their favorite _____.

18. I hit my _____, owww!

19. I like _____; there's no school.

20. The Aliceas go to _____ every Sunday.

Vocabulary Review. See annotation on page 115.

MEMORY BANK

party	milk	nurse	church	sport	many	today
post office		hat	soccer	help	elbow	pen
o'clock	women	summer	hot	supermarket	uncle	notebooks

Vocabulary Review

Complete each sentence with a word from the Memory Bank.

1. Mae Lee is going to the doctor _____ work.

2. Sandra has to take care of the _____ this afternoon.

3. Clean the sink and the _____, please.

4. My girlfriend is a very _____ girl.

5. I don't know the answer to those arithmetic _____.

6. His first name is Carlos and his _____ name is Perez.

7. Andrea is wearing her favorite _____.

8. My favorite breakfast is ham and _____.

9. The door is locked and I don't have the _____.

10. I'm not sick today; I feel _____.

11. Chess is a difficult _____ to learn.

12. I have to _____; my mother is waiting for me.

13. The boys are late; they have to _____ to school.

14. My friends are cooking dinner in the _____.

15. Please don't talk; you are in a _____.

16. Paula's _____ are in the closet.

17. The receptionists have to _____ coffee for the customers.

18. The boys are buying two rock and roll _____.

19. Maria is staying in Los Angeles for one _____.

20. It's hot in here; open the _____.

Vocabulary Review. See annotation on page 115.

MEMORY BANK

library	fine	after	pants	game	dress
key	kitchen	window	go	make	beautiful	baby
bathtub	week	problems	eggs	records	run	last

Vocabulary Review

Complete each sentence with a word from the Memory Bank.

1. Raul isn't walking to school today; he's taking the _____.

2. Don't touch that wall; the paint is _____.

3. I have to wear a _____; these pants are too big.

4. The teacher is _____ because the students are cheating.

5. Mrs. Pena's office is on the third floor of the Tower _____.

6. My plane is _____ soon; I have to say good-bye.

7. They drink _____ at breakfast every morning.

8. His _____ is an excellent athlete.

9. What _____ shoe are you looking for?

10. My hands are cold; where are my _____?

11. The steak is very _____ at this restaurant.

12. I am _____; may I have a drink?

13. In the winter we can _____ on this pond.

14. In the summer, _____ is everyone's favorite dessert.

15. Turn on the _____; I can't see a thing.

16. Mario is home alone; his _____ are away for the day.

17. The _____ is talking to the airport manager.

18. There are a lot of _____ in the store today.

19. I can't eat a large pizza; I want a _____ one, please.

20. I have to go to the dentist; I have a bad _____.

MEMORY BANK

ice cream		tooth	coffee	bus	lamp	angry
size	pilot	daughter	belt	parents	people	gloves
thirsty	wet	Building	small	skate	leaving	expensive

Vocabulary Review

Put the words from the Memory Bank into the correct boxes.

Body Parts	Fruit	Occupations
1. _____	1. _____	1. _____
2. _____	2. _____	2. _____
3. _____	3. _____	3. _____
4. _____	4. _____	4. _____
5. _____	5. _____	5. _____

Clothing	Sports and Games	Family Members
1. _____	1. _____	1. _____
2. _____	2. _____	2. _____
3. _____	3. _____	3. _____
4. _____	4. _____	4. _____
5. _____	5. _____	5. _____

Time Words	Colors
1. _____	1. _____
2. _____	2. _____
3. _____	3. _____
4. _____	4. _____
5. _____	5. _____

━ MEMORY BANK ━

afternoon	black	engineer	lawyer	son
ankle	boots	evening	morning	strawberries
apple	checkers	football	night	suit
architect	chef	granddaughter	noon	swimming
aunt	chess	grapes	pear	throat
banana	chest	gray	purple	thumb
bathrobe	coat	jeans	red	waitress
baseball	cousin	knee	sister	yellow

Vocabulary Review

Put the words from the Memory Bank into the correct boxes.

Musical Instruments	Animals	Weather Words
1. _____	1. _____	1. _____
2. _____	2. _____	2. _____
3. _____	3. _____	3. _____
4. _____	4. _____	4. _____
5. _____	5. _____	5. _____

Furniture	Vegetables	Rooms
1. _____	1. _____	1. _____
2. _____	2. _____	2. _____
3. _____	3. _____	3. _____
4. _____	4. _____	4. _____
5. _____	5. _____	5. _____

Ordinal Numbers	Eating Utensils
1. _____	1. _____
2. _____	2. _____
3. _____	3. _____
4. _____	4. _____
5. _____	5. _____

── MEMORY BANK ──

armchair	cat	drizzling	horse	sofa
bass	clarinet	drums	kitchen	spoon
bathroom	cold	elephant	knife	sunny
beans	corn	fifth	living room	table
bed	cucumber	first	piano	third
bedroom	cup	flute	plate	tiger
bookcase	dining room	fork	potatoes	warm
carrots	dog	fourth	second	windy

Vocabulary Review

A. Match the words in column A with their definitions in column B.

Column A

1. bowl _____
2. eye _____
3. summer _____
4. breakfast _____
5. slippers _____
6. father _____
7. scarf _____
8. winter _____
9. lunch _____
10. ear _____
11. floor _____
12. dinner _____
13. fall _____
14. checkers _____
15. napkin _____
16. tablecloth _____
17. flight attendant _____
18. blouse _____
19. wrist _____
20. slacks _____

Column B

a. comfortable, soft shoes

b. what you walk on indoors

c. round, deep dish for soup or cereal

d. male parent

e. game you play on a red and black board

f. afternoon meal

g. warm and sunny months—June, July, August

h. evening meal

i. cool season—September, October, November

j. airplane worker, stewardess

k. large cloth that you put on a table

l. cloth you wear around your neck

m. woman's shirt

n. part of the body you see with

o. part of the arm where you wear a watch

p. pants, jeans

q. cold season—December, January, February

r. part of the body you hear with

s. morning meal

t. cloth or paper for cleaning mouth and hands

B. Now show that you know what the words mean. Write a complete sentence for each word in Column A. Underline the word you are using. Example: Maria is putting soup in the <u>bowl</u>.

Vocabulary Review. See annotation on page 115.

End of Book Test: Completing Familiar Structures

Circle the best answer.

Example: ___Are___ you going to go to the bank today?

   a. Is   (b. Are)   c. Do   d. Can

1. Liana is here but her sisters _____.

   a. can't   b. isn't   c. don't   d. aren't

2. Bob is _____.

   a. an architect   b. one architect   c. architect   d. architects

3. Francis is living _____ Main Street.

   a. to   b. at   c. on   d. for

4. My brother is listening _____ the news.

   a. to   b. at   c. on   d. for

5. Your socks are _____ the bed.

   a. across from   b. over   c. under   d. next

6. Mr. and Mrs. Jackson _____ the newspaper now.

   a. reading   b. read   c. reads   d. are reading

7. _____ bananas are very good.

   a. These   b. This   c. That   d. Them

8. _____ one hospital in Boxville.

   a. It is   b. There is   c. It has   d. There are

9. Juanita can swim but her brother _____.

   a. isn't   b. don't   c. doesn't   d. can't

10. What's the weather like today? It's _____.

   a. rain   b. to rain   c. raining   d. rains

11. That's John's coat. Please give it to _____.

   a. him   b. his   c. he   d. himself

12. _____'s a sale at Filene's today.

   a. Their   b. The   c. There   d. It

End of Book Test: Completing Familiar Structures (Continued)

Circle the best answer.

13. _____ is she coming?

    a. Where   b. When   c. Who   d. What

14. Why can't Paula come to class? She _____ a bad headache.

    a. has   b. have   c. is   d. having

15. Our vacation is _____ August.

    a. on   b. at   c. for   d. in

16. _____ are they going to do tonight?

    a. What   b. Where   c. What time   d. Why

17. There's an old church _____ the library.

    a. next   b. in front   c. across   d. near

18. Bob and Jill are tired, so I am helping _____.

    a. they   b. them   c. there   d. their

19. Is this your coat? No, it's _____ coat.

    a. Mary   b. Marys   c. hers   d. Mary's

20. What are you _____?

    a. eat   b. to eat   c. eating   d. eats

21. How much _____ those boots?

    a. are   b. is   c. do cost   d. does

22. _____ umbrella is this?

    a. Who's   b. How's   c. What's   d. Whose

23. How _____ airports are there in Dallas?

    a. many   b. much   c. are   d. are there

24. I am looking _____ a new pair of shoes.

    a. from   b. in   c. for   d. on

25. Can you help me? No, I'm sorry. I _____ go to the dentist.

    a. have   b. am   c. going   d. have to

End of Book Test: Writing Questions

Read the sentence. Write the question.

Example: Linda is taking piano lessons at the conservatory.

Where *is Linda taking piano lessons* ?

1. Mario is going to the library at ten o'clock.

When _____ ?

2. They are traveling in Central America now.

Where _____ ?

3. Carlotta is wearing her sister's sweater.

What _____ ?

4. The maid is cleaning the room.

Who _____ ?

5. There are four students from Vietnam in my class.

How many _____ ?

6. No, I'm not happy with my new apartment.

Are _____ ?

7. Carlos is playing volleyball in the park.

Where _____ ?

8. That car is $10,000.

How much _____ ?

9. It's going to rain tonight.

What _____ ?

10. She's crying because she is sad.

Why _____ ?

11. I'm wearing my brother's sneakers.

Whose _____ ?

12. No, Nancy's mother is an engineer.

Is _____ ?

End of Book Test: Writing questions
Go over the directions and example with the class. Point out that the first word(s) of each question is provided. Assign the page as independent work.

End of Book Test: Classifying, Drawing Conclusions

A. Find the matching set of words. Write the letter on the line.

1. clothes _____
2. food _____
3. occupations _____
4. countries _____
5. parts of the body _____
6. months _____
7. furniture _____
8. colors _____
9. family members _____
10. sports _____

a. teacher, lawyer, mechanic, doctor
b. eye, arm, leg, toe
c. red, green, blue, yellow
d. sofa, bed, table, chair
e. basketball, golf, soccer, baseball
f. chicken, apples, milk, carrots
g. daughter, aunt, father, cousin
h. January, February, March, April
i. shirt, hat, coat, socks
j. England, Mexico, Canada, China

B. Find the matching sentence. Write the letter on the line.

1. Carol is a teacher. _____
2. Mr. Black is a pilot. _____
3. He is an engineer. _____
4. She is an astronaut. _____
5. Michel is an actor. _____
6. She is a student. _____
7. Frank is a singer. _____
8. They are nurses. _____
9. They are dancers. _____

a. They are giving medicine.
b. She is flying a space ship.
c. She is writing on the board.
d. They are dancing.
e. He is talking to the workers.
f. He is looking at his plane.
g. He is acting in a play.
h. She is doing her homework.
i. He is singing.

Answer to puzzle on page 87

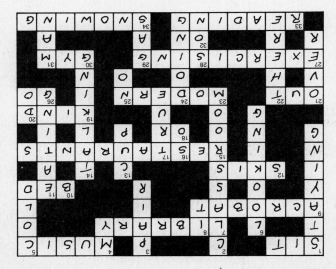

End of Book Test: Classifying, drawing conclusions
Review both sets of directions with the students, then assign as independent work.

End of Book Test: Reading for Details

The Mural

Mrs. Cabral's class is working hard. They are painting a mural outside. A mural is a large picture on a wall. The students are painting their mural on one of the school walls. They are painting a picture of Waverly Street, the main street in their town.

Carlos is painting the buildings. He is painting the bank now. It is between the post office and the supermarket. Rosa and Anh are painting the people. Rosa is working on a picture of Officer Collins, the policeman. Anh is painting a group of schoolchildren. They are playing soccer. Freddy can paint clouds well. He is painting the sky.

Some other students are painting cars, trees, birds, flowers, and houses. They are using bright, pretty colors. Van's favorite color is red. He is painting everything red. There is a red airplane and a red cat in the picture already. The students have to stop Van soon. They want their mural to be beautiful, not funny.

Answer the following quesitons.

1. What is a mural? _____

2. Where are the students painting the mural? _____

3. What are the students painting a picture of? _____

4. Where is the bank? _____

5. Who is Rosa painting? _____

6. Who is Anh painting? _____

7. What can Freddy paint well? _____

8. What are the other students painting? _____

9. What is Van's favorite color? _____

10. Why do the students have to stop Van? _____

Skills Index

The pages listed below are those on which the skills are introduced and/or emphasized. Many of the skills appear, incidentally, on other pages as well.

Grammatical/Structural Skills

Adjectives, 36, 44, 45, 49
  a and an, 59
  possessive adjectives, 23, 44, 48, 49
Nouns
  Count and mass, nouns, 52, 53
  plurals, 52, 53, 78, 84
  possessives('s), 91
Prepositions, 11, 19, 40, 41, 42, 69, 70
Pronouns, 36, 44, 91
There is/are, 77, 78, 79
Verbs
  future form: going to, 94, 95, 96, 97
  have to, has to, 99, 107
  modals: can/can't, 100, 101, 107
  present forms of "to be", 46, 47, 61, 62
  present progressive, 53, 71, 72, 74, 75, 76, 88, 105

Reading Comprehension Skills

Classifying, 31, 56, 58, 70, 102
Drawing conclusions, 95, 99, 109
Drawing inferences, 82, 94, 96, 111, 113
Fact vs. opinion, 81
Following directions, 9, 10, 30, 41, 42
Identifying main idea and details, 26, 36, 43, 82, 96, 97, 113
Identifying topic, 82, 97
Making judgments, 51, 60, 66, 73, 85, 92, 108, 113, 114
Reading for details, 51, 60, 66, 67, 72, 73, 80, 85, 90, 92, 98, 103, 108, 114
Recognizing cause and effect, 86, 104
Sequencing, 19, 76, 105, 110

Reading in the Content Areas

Math
  money: prices and problems, 32, 33, 34, 54, 64
  number names and counting, 14, 77
  ordinal numbers, 20, 112
  time zone math problems, 83
  telling time, 15, 16, 37, 93, 94
Social Studies
  city maps, 41, 42
  community places, 41, 42, 78, 94
  countries and nationalities, 46, 61, 62, 89, 90
  occupations, 13, 61, 62, 63
  U.S. cities and states, 48, 80, 81, 82, 83, 96, 97

Study Skills

Getting information from graphics
  bar graph, 64
  calendar, 19, 20, 112
  diagrams, 70, 71, 103, 104
  family tree, 68
  library card and address form, 24, 25
  maps, 41, 42, 83
  menu, 54
  road signs, 106, 107
  size chart, 30
  time table, 38
Interviewing, 49, 65, 79, 101
Labeling diagrams, 12, 43, 109
Plotting information on maps and charts, 18, 42, 65, 67, 100

Vocabulary Development

Body parts, 109, 110
Clothes, 27, 28
Community places, 41, 42, 78, 94
Countries and nationalities, 61, 62, 89
Days of the week, months, 18, 19, 112
Family members, 67, 68
Feelings, 21, 51, 60, 66, 73, 85, 92, 98, 108, 114
Food, 52, 54, 55, 56, 57
Musical instruments, 74, 100
Occupations, 13, 61, 62, 63
Parts of a bike and car, 103, 104, 105
Rooms and furniture, 70, 71
School vocabulary, 9, 10, 12, 13, 17, 75, 79
Sports and games, 74, 100
Traffic terms, 106, 107
Weather terms, 111

Writing Skills

Autobiographical paragraphs, 26, 48, 100
Descriptions, 29, 36, 45, 50, 61, 62
Descriptive paragraphs, 44, 48, 49, 65, 79, 104
Friendly letters, 50
Informative essays, 90
Negative statements, 47, 67, 72, 78
Questions, 25, 31, 47, 69, 78, 82, 88, 96, 112